On Liberty and Peace

Part One
Liberty

Matt Edge

SOCIETAS
essays in political
& cultural criticism

imprint-academic.com

Copyright © 2010 Matt Edge
The moral rights of the authors have been asserted.
No part of any contribution may be reproduced in any form
without permission, except for the quotation of brief passages
in criticism and discussion.

Published by
Imprint Academic, PO Box 200, Exeter EX5 5YX, UK

Published in the USA by Societas
Imprint Academic, Philosophy Documentation Center
PO Box 7147, Charlottesville, VA 22906-7147, USA

ISBN 9781845402037

A CIP catalogue record for this book is available from the
British Library and US Library of Congress

To My Parents

For teaching me what freedom to judge means
while never being judgemental

Contents

Preface		*vii*
	Introduction	1
1	Liberty	13
2	The Problem of Positive Liberty	33
3	Language, Knowledge, Rationality: The Naturalisation of Political Philosophy	51
4	Conclusion to Part One	108
	Bibliography	120

Preface

Ayer began *Language, Truth and Logic* by saying "the traditional disputes of philosophers are, for the most part, as unwarranted as they are unfruitful."[1] Elisabeth Anscombe began 'Modern Moral Philosophy' by stating "it is not profitable for us at present to do moral philosophy."[2] Even the normally restrained Bernard Williams could write, "most moral philosophy at most times has been empty and boring."[3] I'm afraid that I don't have anything quite so shocking to say, and I don't wish to imply that I belong in such company, or even that I could be called a philosopher. I actually happen to think that much political philosophy (towards which, I have to admit, the present work has pretensions) is spectacularly impressive, though I do hope that this book will try to move the discipline in a different direction, perhaps towards a path it hasn't taken for over 2500 years (though, as I, following a number of others, have said elsewhere, it is perhaps doubtful whether it actually ever took it then).

The political philosophy of this book might be called participatory. Not only am I a passionate believer in participatory democracy, I am also concerned with how political philosophy can be participatory, which might be another way for saying accessible. It is a central argument of the following that political philosophy is, or should be, as important to you (and everyone else) as the subjects which seem to define our (or perhaps any) age – the movement of the planets, the way our human bodies function and the changing physical and natural world around us. Believe me when I say that this book

---

[1] Ayer 2001, p. 13.
[2] Anscombe 1997, p. 26.
[3] Williams 1972, p. 9.

is about you (and everyone else), far more than it is about me and only you (and everyone else) can say whether or not I have lived up to my claims about accessibility.

If this book is intended to launch a debate, then let me begin with a plea as to how that debate is conducted. I think that many people are put off, certainly modern politics, and possibly modern political theory as well, by personal invective and polemical claims to subjective truth. Doubtless I will fail to live up to my own ideals, and I particularly regret that the second half of chapter three seems far more polemical than I had intended, but I don't think any debate can get very far unless it is conducted with open ears, open hearts and open minds, with a genuine willingness to listen, accompanied by a genuine acknowledgement that you or I (or both), the disputants, may be wrong. It seems strange to begin a project with an open acknowledgement that the answer it provides may be wrong, but since, as readers will hopefully soon see, this is representative of the very essence of what I am arguing in these pages. It seems, on the contrary, a fully appropriate place at which to begin. However, before beginning that debate, let me say a few words of thanks.

I must start by thanking a large number of people who have helped with the development of my ideas, and who have supported me through thick and thin. Malcolm Schofield and Janet Coleman provided keen criticism of some of these embryonic ideas, and the latter has particularly been a constant source of inspiration and encouragement to me over the past few years. The same should be said of Ryan Balot, with whom I have benefitted from a number of exchanges which have helped to greatly clarify my thinking on a number of points. I must also thank Ian Malcolm for his kindness and for some interesting discussions about my work. Claire Grant has also read my work and offered a number of interesting comments which have directed me – indeed – towards new directions. My former students, in Nottingham and Cambridge, were vital in the development of my thinking and it was an absolute privilege to have been taught by each and every one of them.

To my friends, Harry Platanakis, Kostas Vlassopoulos, Aleka Lianeri, Eftychia Bathrellou and Anthony Miller, I owe

Preface

thanks for countless interesting exchanges, over countless interesting evenings, and all of them have greatly contributed to the development of my thought and have each encouraged me and supported me for many years. Words cannot express the debt I owe them. David Jacobs kindly lent his keen eye for detail to proofreading this manuscript and for this I remain hugely grateful.

Going a little further back, Steve Hodkinson and Stephen Todd were hugely supportive of me, and encouraging to me, in the years when I first encountered Athenian democracy, and I will never forget the wisdom, insight and passion they imparted to me. Going further back still, I must thank Sheilagh Hughes and Lucy Hare for showing me a patience I simply did not deserve. *Without Whom Not* as they say.

To John Salmon, I owe thanks for companionship and inspiration over many fascinating discussions about Athenian democracy. John is as inspiring a man as he is a teacher and I will never forget his kindness and inspiration.

To Quentin Skinner, I owe thanks for both inspiration from his work and for his kindness and generosity towards mine. I sent him a copy of this manuscript as a fervent disciple in the hope that he might offer comments and encouragement. He read, and commented on it, within twenty four hours and has provided encouragement ever since. He will remain a constant inspiration to me, as much for his kindness as his innovative and passionate approach to political philosophy and its history which, as will be clear from the following, has had a huge bearing on the development of my thought.

It seems strange to thank someone I have never met, nor had any contact with, but I cannot fail to mention the late Donald Davidson, whose work has had a profound influence on the development of my thought and in a number of ways. Not only was Davidson a brilliant and remarkable philosopher, reading his work also strikes me as the way debates should be conducted – in a warm, accessible and charitable, yet passionate fashion – a mood and tone which I will certainly try, though in all likelihood fail, to emulate. This is confirmed by Richard Rorty's kind review of one of Davidson's final collection of essays, which I mention in the text. Rorty also notes there that Davidson's work has dropped off undergraduate philosophy reading lists. Given the importance of his radical and innovative approach to philosophy, I can only hope this changes. I have no idea what Davidson would have made of my own work, but that is not reason enough not to thank him for months, of inspiring reading which have – very literally – revealed a new way of looking at the world to me.

To Paul Cartledge, what can I say? He was an inspiring supervisor and has remained an inspiring mentor ever since. Paul is one of the most accessible and approachable people I have ever met, only equalled, in fact, by the accessibility and approachability of his work, which remains a constant inspiration to me for this very reason, and for many others besides. Likewise, Paul's kindness is only matched by the encyclopedic knowledge he brings to his work, as anyone who has been fortunate enough to meet him, or work alongside him, will testify. He has read countless drafts of this manuscript, and many others besides, and improved every one immeasurably with an unmatched eye for detail and a similarly unmatched command of interesting facts, further reading and further and future directions. He has provided constant encouragement and support when I have most needed it and was also the one who directed me towards Imprint Academic, a piece of advice for which I will remain eternally grateful.

At Imprint, Anthony Freeman has been an incredibly patient and understanding editor and has been a pleasure to work with. I must also thank, in particular, an anonymous reader for Imprint who produced a lengthy report on my work which has helped me improve it in immeasurable ways. I can genuinely say that this was the most helpful review process I have yet been through and I cannot thank she or he more than that. Imprint's designer has also done an incredible job of capturing the essence of what this project is about.

My friends and family have also been a constant source of support and encouragement through the difficult days. My colleagues, in Leicester, Coventry and Chelmsley Wood, over the past three years, who I won't name (you all know who you are), are a constant source of inspiration through their passion and dedication to their work. My partner, Katie Jacobs, has the capacity to endure my frustrations and endless ramblings about freedom and peace in a way I never thought possible. And my parents, to whom I dedicate this work as a small token of gratitude for everything they have done for me over the past 30 years, brought me up to judge freely and to question everything I saw around me, whilst also constantly reminding me, in small but vital ways, of the hopeful human condition which, ultimately, lies in all of us.

Any mistakes are and remain my own, but I owe a huge debt of gratitude to all the above (and many more besides) for helping me address previous flaws. None of my opinions, of course, can be taken as representing anyone I have mentioned, but I must thank each and every one of them for propelling me, and accompanying me, along the journey which has led me to those opinions. And that, to bring us finally full circle, is what, in short, has led me to you ...

Matt Edge
Leicester, November 2009

Introduction

The hardest thing is knowing where to begin. I have found this truism is somewhat amplified when the two concepts employed in my title are involved, so vast and amorphous they are.

I should perhaps begin with an admission, though not I hope, an admission of guilt of any kind. This project is deliberately situated on the margins. That is to say at the intersection where political philosophy meets other disciplines, notably ethics, philosophy of language and epistemology, and history (among others). I hope it will immediately become clear from this introduction why it is I believe these diverse disciplines are actually a great deal closer to one another than we might at first think, and why we might need to employ them all in the same enterprise.

To begin with political philosophy, it seems impossible, at the outset, to avoid mentioning the name of John Rawls, the most influential political theorist of our time and a man whose work (particularly *A Theory of Justice*) has influenced people from all the disciplines I have mentioned and many more besides.[1] I do not personally believe, as I will go on to argue, that Rawls always provided us with the right answers, but he certainly sets the questions (as well as the standard). And I mean that very literally.

There are, I believe, two fundamental – and naturally interrelated – questions of political philosophy. The first, to paraphrase Rawls,[2] is how are we to create and secure conditions for peaceful social cooperation over time? The

---
[1] Rawls 1999a [1971] is his most influential work, but Rawls 1996, 1999b and 2001 are also very important. I refer to other works throughout.
[2] E.g. Rawls 2001, § 2.1 p. 5.

second is: how much liberty[3] can we each expect to enjoy as human beings living at a particular moment of historical time engaged in the enterprise described by the first question? I do not deny that these constructions beg an awful lot of questions (particularly perhaps, concerning how they relate to one another) but I hope I will be forgiven that for the moment (though only for the moment). The important matters as to why liberty and peace (and related concepts) *are* (or could be) important, are dealt with in the main text(s).

In brief, this project sets out to firstly (in part one), provide a structure, or a groundwork, by which these questions can be answered and, secondly (in part two), to give an actual answer to them. This is where the two titular concepts come in. Part one is concerned with liberty and part two – principally – with peace. I will here, just give a brief outline of how the structure (built in part one) will look, but not the reasons for it.

Rawls constructed an ingenious device – actually a number of ingenious devices – by which to answer these (and a number of other) questions.[4] He started by looking at the "public political culture of a democratic society"[5] for its traditions, structures, institutions and values. I'll say something more about this in a moment, but moving on, Rawls used certain of those values to construct a political conception of justice which he believed rational human beings, under a 'veil of ignorance' from his famous 'original position', would accept.

Let me point out that readers will notice (in places) what might appear to be a very Rawlsean structure to the theory I attempt to sketch in this project, even though my approach and my answer is very different from Rawls'. I don't deal in original positions and veils of ignorance – quite the contrary – but the starting point (and at least part of the basic philosophical structure) is the same and it is important

---

[3] Or 'freedom'. I use the two terms interchangeably throughout.
[4] This is only a very brief survey and it in no way does justice to the complexity of Rawls' analysis. Rawls' arguments are dealt with in greater detail throughout my project, although I should point out that it is not my specific purpose to provide an answer to, or a sustained critique of, Rawls. Instead, I try to go beyond Rawls in a slightly different way.
[5] Rawls 2001, § 2.1 p. 5. And see also the important n. 5 p. 5 which elaborates on a worry about this.

to point this out at the very beginning. This said however, it is equally important to acknowledge that Rawls' aim and mine, are fundamentally different.

I say I don't deal in original positions and veils of ignorance so let me say why. I follow Rawls in that, during the process I will describe, we must look to those successful concepts and values which make sense to us as human beings engaged in such a project of ongoing societal co-operation over time, i.e. those values and concepts that are most 'human' and are accepted (and acceptable) as such.[6] We must then try to establish the political structures, systems and institutions which best realise those values. Two of these are 'liberty', and 'peace', although other concepts, 'equality' and 'justice' in particular, will have similarly important roles in what follows. This may well lead us down paths that realise very different structures from the ones we now inhabit (if they don't happen to measure up to those openly professed values),[7] but that is a worry I'll return to later.

Now, one question that immediately arises from all this is, *who* decides what political, economic and social structures (defined and set up by certain laws, institutions and the like), *suggested* by those fundamental principles, values or concepts, we are to establish? Answers have typically been that it should be a man, or a certain body of men (and historically, regrettably, I do mean men and we must recognise and confront that and the deep and negative influence it still has on society), who are thought to have a certain level of intelligence or understanding of political (as well as perhaps, other) matters above that of the rest of us. This thought has been all-pervasive, especially so in Western culture,[8] and it still remains – prominently – with us, though I'm glad to say that it no longer remains gender-specific.[9]

---

[6] There is a problem with this. There may well be alternative meanings (uses) of those concepts currently in use in everyday linguistic communication and, therefore, our language-picture might not be as accurate in this regard as it appears. This is a major problem and it forms a large part of the argument of part one.
[7] Cf. Skinner 1998, pp. 78–79.
[8] See, for example, Edge (Forthcoming A).
[9] Cf. the well-aimed conclusion to Cartledge 2009, pp. 136–137.

This project provides a very different answer. In short, I argue that it should be each of us togther, deciding and that no one should be doing it for us. This means placing the judging of those two fundamental questions of political philosophy I have just mentioned back into our own hands. Far from being an ahistorical, otherworldly, 'original position', hypothetical situation or device of representation, this is, to the contrary, construed as a real, empirical, moment in historical time starting from *now*. This clearly means radical changes in the way both political philosophy and politics in general is done, and I will return to this below. I also argue that we are more than capable of successfully resolving this undertaking, indeed we (the men and women who collectively constitute 'the people') might be even more capable of it than those men and women who currently do it on our behalf (though they generally do it in a more restricted, legislative, sense than the structure I am imagining). This is still begging a lot of questions, but since I am outlining the structure of the project, I'm afraid that will have to remain the case for the time being.

I said Rawls' aim and mine were different. As Rawls says,

> to argue from a given list [of conceptions of justice] cannot, of course, establish what is the most appropriate conception of justice among all possible alternatives, the best conception, as it were. It may, however, suffice for our first and minimum objective: namely, to find a conception of political justice that can specify an appropriate moral basis of democratic institutions and can hold its own against the known existing alternatives.[10]

My ultimate aim is to propose a project of peace which I believe *is* the most suitable conception of justice and is acceptable to human beings as such – and in this first part, to urge others (so far as this has not already been done) to propose similar projects of peace and justice.[11] This is providing that justice is

---
[10] Rawls 2001, § 23.4 p. 83.
[11] These, I am assuming, will be based on different answers to the questions I began with, i.e. different descriptions of the amount of liberty to be provided to human beings under a variety of different social conditions and with that, how far those bundles of freedom are to be equal. This is discussed throughout the present text.

defined, as in Rawls,[12] as the principles which will define the fair means of social cooperation for human beings living in society over time.

The aim gets still more ambitious, which may be a good thing, depending, as Leonard Cohen liked to say, on your politics. By this I mean that the principles I put forward in part two of this project[13] relate not (solely) to those of us who live in a modern democratic nation-state, but as individuals who are part, in the cosmopolitan sense, of a global order which is, in modern times, defined by global interaction, global productivity and global need. It is also a globe of conflict. However, what perhaps the greatest modern projects of perpetual peace from the Abbé St. Pierre through to Bentham and Kant and, in our day, Rawls and Habermas, have not understood, or at least not confronted, very well is that these conflicts take place not solely between nation-states and as national civil wars, but they also occur in much deeper, more material, immediate and immanent ways. They take place, in other words, on street corners and city-centres, between ourselves and between our closest neighbours, in our workplaces and factories, at borders and in places of leisure throughout every land on the earth. And all of these conflicts undermine the ongoing attempts at cooperation over time. This is where projects for perpetual peace – or perhaps, universal justice – should be aimed.

Some might wish to immediately dismiss this as utopian. I will come back to this issue later, and (particularly) in part two, but I think utopianism is a lazy charge to apply to such a difficult task or question. The task may be difficult, may ultimately prove to be too difficult, though how anyone can lay claim to knowing that before the task itself is attempted remains beyond me. As Quentin Skinner puts it,

> I have never understood why the charge of utopianism is necessarily thought to be an objection to a theory of politics. One legitimate aspiration of moral and political theory is surely to show us what lines of action we are committed to undertaking by the values we profess to accept.[14]

---

[12] E.g., Rawls 1996, § 1 p. 4; 1999a, p. 10.
[13] Henceforward referred to as Edge (Forthcoming C)
[14] Skinner 1998, pp. 78–79.

A Cursory Summary

In short, this is a very brief summary of the essential structure I put forward in the pages that follow. I envisage a moment in historical time – starting from *now* – when each of us is given the choice (from a number of competing alternatives) as to how we are to successfully live under conditions of peaceful cooperation over time and, concomitantly, how much liberty we can expect to enjoy whilst doing so, during (in Jefferson's famous phrase) "our pursuit of happiness over a complete life". In short, as in Rawls' theory – but in a very different way and for a very different purpose[15] – we are selecting, from a number of competing alternatives, the conception of justice, or the form of social organism described by that conception, we consider the best one, which will promote human and, therefore, our happiness in the most effective and genuinely sustainable way. This is, as I say, no hypothetical 'original position' but rather, an actual real moment in historical time, which it is (part of) the purpose of this book to seek to bring about.[16] So we select that concept of justice, or the set of political, economic and social arrangements described by that conception, from the actual list of alternatives which writers put on the table. These will range from the present system (and all its variants, some left, some right), through anarchism, communism, socialism and conservatism, together with other forms of social organism we are yet to conceive of, assuming that these are possible, and all the other forms of social organism which I have not included in this list.

Since it is a real moment of historical time, with real historical actors – there can be (and ought, anyway, not to be) a 'veil of ignorance' preventing us from knowing what our interests and instincts are. We have interests, feelings, thoughts and instincts and we need them, since they will provide us with many important tools (and clues) for performing this

---

[15] See Rawls 2001, § 23.4 p. 83.
[16] I have more to say about the (obvious) problems and challenges this brings about later. I hope that it is, at least, clear that I am not so arrogant, or so naive, to expect that the publication of this book will bring about an immediate, seamless and radical change in modern political life. Yet, as I say, there are a number of interesting questions related to issues of publication, influence, authority and change which I will have to address later. See pp. 98–107 below.

task to the best of our abilities, particularly around what it is rational for us to do and choose. If (as is partly the case in Rawls' story) we could somehow be unaware of what we are as human beings, of what we need, like, intend, want and enjoy (and also of what causes us to conflict with one another), we necessarily lose a large part of our understanding of our motivation and of the conditions under which our behaviour is to be guided. Freedom could suffer hugely as a result.[17]

Clearly this is not going to be easy and at no point do I assume that it will be. Looking around us now, at the end of the first decade of the second millennium, a situation such as the one I have outlined where we, the people, are given the real material, practical choice between a number of differing and competing political (and other) structures, is clearly a long way off. Further, if this task were suddenly thrust upon us: or, more correctly, if we did decide this was an important enterprise to collectively undertake,[18] we would not be in a position to do it to the best of our abilities and, importantly, to do it freely, for the reasons I shall discuss below. If we are to have a genuine free choice between competing alternatives (on all levels, social, political, economic and so on), then other systems from the ones we currently inhabit must be shown to us to be reliable and realisable, a genuinely available choice to human beings making rational judgements.

It must then be the task of those who ascribe to such systems to lay them out clearly and honestly and to argue not only that their conception, or the society described by that conception, is the most just form of social organism, but also the one most rational for each of us to accept. Here, political philosophy clearly has a vital role to play and this is exactly what I set out to achieve in part two, that is to argue on behalf of those systems and structures I believe will be most conducive to human well-being and dignity, because they

---

[17] And, besides, since we are all doing it ourselves without representatives (who *could*, plausibly, be ignorant of their constituents' choices and of what they want) it would be impossible without some totalitarian style mindwashing device that doesn't even bear contemplation.
[18] If this clause in parentheses is not added then the whole structure itself becomes coercive and oppressive, thereby having immediate negative implications for freedom and for the theory of freedom I sketch in part one.

successfully establish certain cherished values (liberty and peace among them) in certain ways.

Part one only argues on behalf of setting up these conditions (and can therefore be read as a free-standing essay on liberty) but part two is an active, subjective, intervention in the debate itself, necessarily building on the theoretical structure outlined in part one.

I'll just say a little bit more here about the content of parts one and two and their context. Part one, as I have said, outlines a free-standing theory of individual liberty. It stems from a wish to answer certain aspects of Isaiah Berlin's seminal essay 'Two Concepts of Liberty',[19] which retains a huge amount of influence over the subject. My theory of freedom is based around a solution to the problem of positive freedom which Berlin uncovered, but in my view, did not correctly or fully diagnose. The radical democratic structure I propose is, I argue, the natural way out of the dangers Berlin saw as being at the heart of positive liberty doctrines.[20] This will surprise a few people familiar with Berlin's essay and with the literature that has followed it. As I point out later, radical, participatory democracy has, since Berlin, generally been viewed as the exemplification of positive conceptions of freedom and certainly not as the natural way out of the problems posed by Berlinean positive freedom. It will be my task to demonstrate that these analyses, by linking participatory accounts of democracy to Berlinean positive freedom, have overlooked this and have therefore missed a potential solution to the problem.

As a corollary of this, part one stresses the importance of Donald Davidson's approach to the philosophy of language and epistemology to the discipline of political philosophy in general (as I conceive of it here). Meanings of words, and how we come to learn the meanings of those words (i.e. the social context in which we learn and its accompanying beliefs, views, prejudices and assumptions), are key to both understanding our world and to how we might change it. How, for example, it shapes our liberty and how the degrees of liberty we enjoy might be altered. The Davidsonian theory of triangulation (of

---

[19] Berlin 2002b.
[20] Cf. Edge (Forthcoming A).

speaker, hearer and outside world[21]) in the learning process is both key to political philosophy in general and to the question of liberty in particular.[22] Meaning and (the highly complex process of) knowledge acquisition are key to our performing the kind of task I have laid out here and discuss in full in the pages that follow.

I have already said a bit about this in relation to rational and free choice from a number of competing alternatives, but there are other aspects to this story that can be as basic as learning an alternative meaning to a word we employ in everyday linguistic communication. For example, as Quentin Skinner has demonstrated with his discussions of the neo-classical concept of freedom,[23] the uncovering or excavating, of other possibly long-dead (or long-hidden) means of employing our fundamental normative concepts can have two effects. Not only can it begin to introduce us to a different possible world (rejected at a given moment of historical time), it can also, just as importantly, "help to liberate us from the grip of any one hegemonal account of those values and how they should be interpreted and understood."[24] The acquisition of new meanings or uses available to us to learn and internalise, is, then, fundamentally connected to the problems around rationality I have outlined and many others besides. Equally, in relation to the problem of positive freedom I have mentioned (as I will explain in full below), it can help us to see that the world we inhabit is not a neutral one, nor a political, social and economic structure that is the inevitable result of neutral historical forces.

I do not believe Davidson's work has had the influence on political philosophy it might have done,[25] and I hope this project will go some way towards showing how a Davidsonian approach to language and epistemology (and related issues such as rationality) is vital to political philosophy in general.

---

[21] Or, teacher, learner and outside world, or interpreter, subject and outside world (and so on).
[22] Full references are given in part one but, for now, see, for example, Davidson 2001b, pp. 205–220.
[23] Discussed in full below.
[24] Skinner 1998, p. 117.
[25] One obvious exception is the work of Quentin Skinner, though not principally from the type of perspective I sketch in part one.

Part two moves on (finally) to try and construct a comprehensive answer to those two fundamental questions of political philosophy I have mentioned and won't again repeat. It, then, seeks to build on the theory sketched in part one. It is, therefore, a deliberate and fully subjective intervention in the debate (or discussion) called for (and launched) in part one.

It argues, from a cosmopolitan perspective, on behalf of the kind of conditions that would be required to form a lasting and desirable peace among human beings on earth, and of the amount of freedom we could (and should) expect to enjoy under such conditions. In this way, it can be read as an updating of Immanuel Kant's famous essay 'Towards Perpetual Peace: A Philosophical Sketch'.[26] A clue to my argument is provided by its subtitle, 'A Material Sketch'. I argue, as I have said, that peace amongst human beings will not be established unless focus is placed on the everyday material relationships between individual human beings and groups of human beings and not solely on the relationships between different nation-states on the global stage. Unlike Kant (and those who have followed him[27]), who focused on the global structures that may (or may not) secure peace among conflicting nation-states, we must focus on these everyday, fundamental relationships between individual human beings, not solely those between nation-states (and would-be nation states). A far more exacting notion of 'peace' – focused on individual to individual (as well as on nation-state to nation-state) interaction – needs to be considered if universal justice and perpetual peace are to be established.

The starting point is again Rawlsian. In *Political Liberalism*, Rawls identified that a conception of justice must be political, not comprehensive or metaphysical.[28] In a modern, cosmopolitan, democracy, citizens have competing conceptions

---

[26] Kant 1996.
[27] I have in mind here particularly Habermas 1997 and Rawls 1999b, who argue, as Kant did, for transformations and reforms in the way nation-states relate to one another (prominent today are such themes as the strengthening of global courts of justice, the strengthening and reform of the UN, global tax redistributions and the like). It is my argument that such ideas do not go (nearly) far enough.
[28] See Rawls 1996, pp. 11–13, for example; Rawls 1999c.

Introduction

of the good and, if they are to live together with one another under conditions of peaceful co-operation over time, then it will be necessary to order society according to a freestanding 'political' conception of justice, which does not sponsor any one single comprehensive moral doctrine as to how human beings should live their lives.[29] As Rawls puts it, how is it possible that there may exist over time a stable and just society of free and equal citizens profoundly divided by reasonable though incompatible religious, philosophical and moral doctrines?"[30] The idea then, is to find a political conception of justice which is acceptable to an 'overlapping consensus' of human beings each with competing comprehensive conceptions of the good.[31]

This is the aim of part two – to propose my own answer to this question to see if it is acceptable to you (and everyone else) as the fairest, and best, means of ordering society over time. It will be this then, I shall argue, which will help to establish perpetual peace among human beings, or as close to that as we can hope and indeed want to get. In other words, this is an appeal (like Rawls' own *Law of Peoples*[32]) not solely to a modern, cosmopolitan, democratic nation-state, but to a globalised social order of which I count myself a fortunate member.

Therefore, I propose those principles of justice which I believe will provide both the most rational, and the most just, or fair, answer to the questions I began with. In other words, I propose a structure (which I shall term 'egalitarian equal liberty') which argues that the amount of freedom it provides for its (would be) inhabitants, and the degree to which it equalises that freedom, will also provide conditions for a lasting, sustainable and desirable peace on earth. And, remember, I make no judgement on how you perceive these matters, on whether you do so as a rational egoist or an altruistic saint or both.

The appeal is to both aspects of humanity, the rational and the moral (so far as the two are distinct) and the judgement

---

[29] See, especially, Rawls 1996, pp. xviii–xx.
[30] Rawls 1996, pp. 3–4.
[31] Ibid.
[32] Rawls 1999b.

is yours to make on the grounds you (and everyone else) do, indeed, judge such matters. Most importantly, I make no claim that the structure I will provide constitutes 'true liberty' and, therefore, the society that should be imposed upon everyone because it realises your deepest, most rational and harmonious interests, no matter how deeply you might reject it and struggle against it.[33] It is simply for you and everyone else to decide whether or not you agree for I, just like any other subjective political theorist or writer putting a proposal forward into the arena of intersubjective communication,[34] may be wrong.

This is the project's basic structure. Part two is my own intervention in the debate I call for, according to the structure I outline in part one, but at no point am I remotely claiming that it is the only, or true answer or possibility (or groundwork). Nor am I claiming that the *uses* of the normative concepts I employ, 'liberty', 'equality', 'democracy' and 'peace' prominent amongst them, are the correct, true, or only meanings (uses), that my 'true' conceptual scheme should replace the false one we are currently duped by.[35] The project I put forward in part two might well be rejected (and there are a number of reasons why it might be), but the point is that we all be given the opportunity to reject it, alongside other projects and systems (to be laid out by others, hopefully in response to what I have to say here). Given the free choice, we might even reject the platform I outline below, but to do that, we must be given the 'free choice' in the first instance and this, as I have said, means focusing on the meaning of 'free' here as much as 'choice'. This again, is where language and rationality come in.

I hope the book could be the beginning of a different kind of political philosophy, of a participatory and empowering political philosophy done by, and accessible to, all of us (so far as what we might do could, or should, be called political philosophy) but, even if it is successful, it could never, as the last sentences of part one try to show, be more than a beginning. I hope that the approach I suggest will be a new and enlightening one in this post-Rawlsean world we inhabit. And since that takes me back to Rawls and my beginning, it seems only fitting that, for now, I should end there.

---

[33] See pp. 32 ff. below.
[34] See, especially, pp. 61–69 below.
[35] See Edge (Forthcoming C).

Chapter One
Liberty

The Importance of Human Freedom

So, why is liberty[37] of fundamental importance to human beings? The answer in short, is that conditions of freedom provide us with the necessary opportunities for (in Jefferson's famous words) "the pursuit of happiness" over a complete life. Liberty provides the means for exploring the world, the peoples and individuals within it, and all the cultural artefacts (foods, clothing, practices, religions, objects and symbols etc.) which are available through the vast amount of human diversity across the planet and, therefore, for exploring ourselves, for doing our own good in our own way while, concomitantly, we discover what that (on a vast number of levels) might actually entail.

When constructing an (or any) analysis of a new or an existing social organism, freedom is likely to be the concept we do best with, and this is something the great liberal writers can justifiably say that they have understood better than most. This is precisely because they realised that an account of liberty should not reflect any one conception of the good – Rawls' work particularly perhaps, as it evolved into *Political Liberalism*,[38] is one recent and effective example of this. As expressed by the second of the two constructions I began with, we are, then, seeking the greatest possible amount of pure, undirected liberty, which allows all (and I do mean all) to pursue their own conceptions of the good in accordance with a like amount for others. This has to be in a sustainable functioning form of human society, as the greatest writers on peace realised, since under conditions of brutality, conflict, want, oppression and

---
[37] Or 'freedom', I use the terms interchangeably throughout.
[38] See, for example, Rawls 1996, pp. xviii ff.

deprivation, human freedom is so reduced as to be almost worthless, if not totally annihilated.

Liberty is the only concept that can do this. This is not to say that other concepts, such as (indeed), 'peace', 'equality' and 'justice', are not equally vital in any overarching account of a political organism, but this does help to illustrate the role that liberty plays which no other concept can play.

This is because liberty provides the basis for toleration. If I agree for you to have this (x) amount of freedom, where you are to be left alone to go your own way and do your own thing, then you might agree to do the same for me, and so on. For, in a modern, cosmopolitan, global order, where each of us has competing conceptions of what is good or important in life, if we are all to live together harmoniously, amongst the multiplicity of competing life-plans, we cannot start imposing our own versions of the good for all to follow.[39]

The concept of freedom, then, provides the beginning for an account of how we might be able to live together successfully in lasting and sustainable cooperation over time. It provides the basis for saying how I, an atheist, can live in harmony and social cooperation with a Christian, a Muslim, a Buddhist, a Sikh (and so on), each with our own conceptions of the good (if indeed, each of us has one).

What this does not yet do is provide an account of how much freedom it is right or fair or, indeed, in our interests, to give up (and why). This is essentially what I am suggesting that we are deciding in the participatory project I am proposing – in other words, how much freedom we need to give up, and why, and how far these individual bundles of freedom can, and should, be equalised. The benefit of my project is that it is – precisely – us who are deciding this and that we are not leaving it to someone else to do on our behalf.[40] However, these last few paragraphs point to themes which must wait to be developed as they beg a number of questions, so I will not (generally) return to them here. I mention these issues here because it is important to acknowledge the structure we are considering (and developing) from the very beginning.

---

[39] Cf. Rawls 1996, pp. xviii ff. This is taken up further in Edge (Forthcoming C).
[40] See chapter 2.

One further point needs also to be given particular stress. When I speak of liberty, I speak of it as a human, not a Western value.[41] What matters, when we speak of liberty, is the open doors, the available opportunities, the paths down which to walk, not walking down a particular, 'true', path to (so-called) "true freedom".[42] Part of this may be that I want to enjoy my free time sitting in my chair, reading comics and watching horror films. Or, it may equally be that I wish to live under the stricter moral code of a given religion, which (in some ways) might actually limit my freedom of choice, because it enjoins greater duties regarding my relationships with my fellow human beings, according to the moral principles of benevolence and compassion, for example. The point is that nothing, or no one, forces me to make that choice, that I make it freely and willingly, according to the dictates of my natural character and natural emotional development. Now, this makes what we mean by 'natural character' and its cognates a very important – and difficult – question, but regrettably it is not one I will be able to address here, for lack of space.[43] Liberty entails the doing of my own good in my own way, choosing the routes that please me and doing the things I enjoy, building the relationships that make me happy, and so on. If the choices I make are fully my choices, and they are choices made from a number of viable, possibly even conflicting alternatives, who are you to tell me that I am unfree in making them, that I am making myself a slave by doing so?

Freedom is fundamentally a concept of degree, which each of us possesses in greatly differing degrees. Further, in the kind of structure I am proposing, each different form of social organism (from pure anarchism to watchful conservatism) will propose social conditions with greatly differing degrees of individual liberty and, indeed, how and to what degree those pockets of individual freedom should be equal. If, that is, thinkers from across the political spectrum do indeed contribute such proposals and I shall come back to this. However, an unbounded degree of liberty (for, say, a given

---

[41] To put it a slightly different way, 'liberty' ought not to be confused (as it often is) with living in a capitalistic, representative, liberal democracy. I shall shortly come back to this point.
[42] Cf. below, on 'positive liberty.'
[43] See Edge (Forthcoming D).

individual) would mean the opportunity to do, to explore and to use anything and everything on the planet (and even beyond it, if we include things that are currently beyond our means as a species, or perhaps, just within our means). The last sentence in parentheses also points to the fact that liberty is evolutionary. As we develop as a species, more objects and therefore, more choices and opportunities, will be made available to us through technological, scientific, emotional, educational and (many) other developments. Compare the current opportunities for today's generations (video games, television, the Internet, new educational devices and choices, new careers to pursue, the list goes on) with those available in Victorian times (say)[44], not to mention that human liberty can itself, fundamentally, be preserved and lengthened by medical advances.

Human Freedom

Let me briefly return to one of those constructions I began with. How much liberty can I expect to enjoy while living in a sustainable human society over time, amongst millions, even billions, of other human beings expecting to enjoy the same? It will shortly be time to delve straight into the many controversies raised by this question and related issues – particularly, perhaps, around the question of how much we can expect our respective areas, or realms, of liberty (yours, mine and everyone else's) to be equal and to what degree (and why)[45] – but some controversies must wait until part two. Here, generally, I leave aside the issues raised by the awkward (and elusive) phrase 'sustainable human society', since I believe that, if we are to stand any hope of answering this question, in both a genuine and a just way, we must begin from the beginning, with the concept of freedom itself. My argument in the following pages centres around this simple idea. By doing so, I hope to prepare the groundwork for answering this question on its own terms. For instance, once a groundwork (of a kind) is complete, then other concepts

---

[44] Moral evolution and development is important in just this way too. Compare the freedom for homosexuals now (even if it is far from perfect) from what it was in Victorian Britain. I should also point out, however, that certain freedoms (whether desirable or not) can also be lost, as well as gained.
[45] See, especially, pp. 108–119 below.

– such as equality, peace and justice – can begin to enter our story as they begin to do here.

So, then, it must now be time to stop begging questions and getting down to the key issues at hand. What does 'liberty' *mean*? The most normal sense implied in the word is, as Berlin correctly analysed,[46] an absence of control over my life. My 'liberty' is the area in which I am free to move and choose, without prevention, control, hindrance, bullying, coercion and intimidation by others, or, as I shall argue, by conditions and structures. It is the choices and opportunities that are open to me, the paths available to me to walk, the doors that are open before me, which I can (in a real and genuine way) choose to open (or not). Let me quote from Berlin, arguably the most celebrated of modern defenders of individual liberty.

> The extent of my social or political freedom consists in the absence of obstacles not merely to my actual, but to my potential choices – to my acting in this way or that if I choose to do so. Similarly absence of such freedom is due to the closing of such doors or failure to open them, as a result, intended or unintended, of alterable human practices, of the operation of human agencies.[47]

There is, already, in these few sentences, a good deal of controversy.

For a start, it is a vital part of the argument of this essay to suggest that when we are speaking about my 'freedom to do something' this includes, not just the theoretical area left to me by my government and the laws of the society I live in (and the 'rights' that protect it),[48] but those practical, material choices that are genuinely available to me through the conditions, and the situation, in which I live. When I come to make a choice,

---

[46] Berlin 2002b, pp. 169 with ff. See also Nelson 2005, esp. pp. 73–74. This is discussed further in Edge (Forthcoming B).
[47] Berlin 2002b, p. 32. Not that this statement is empty of controversy, not least the innocent looking 'alterable human practices'. I will discuss some of these controversies later.
[48] This should, of course, read, by the *absence* of governmental control, laws, decrees and statutes. It is this 'negative' area, this absence (as it were), which is protected by basic rights and other constitutional guarantees. These are supposed to mark the absolute line which the government is (supposedly) not to cross.

I am limited to the number of genuinely available paths, opportunities or options open to me.[49] Or, to put it a little better, the sum of my liberty is the sum of those choices, those opportunities, that are genuinely open to me to make, or not to make (regardless, of course, of whether or not I have ever thought about wanting to make those choices).

Berlin argues the contrary. "It is important to discriminate," he says, "between liberty and the conditions of its exercise."[50]

Berlin goes on to say

> This is not merely pedantic distinction, for if it is ignored, the meaning and value of *freedom of choice* is apt to be downgraded. In their zeal to create social and economic conditions in which alone freedom is of genuine value, men tend to forget freedom itself; and if it is remembered, it is liable to be pushed aside to make room for those other values with which the reformers or revolutionaries have become preoccupied.[51]

So that I will not be accused of being unfair, Berlin, I think, makes the root of this distinction clear elsewhere. "I am normally said to be free to the degree to which no man or body of men interferes with my activity. *Political* liberty in this sense is simply the area within which a man can act unobstructed by others" (my italics).[52]

The addition of the word 'political' here is to perform, I would argue, just the kind of "sleight of hand" which Berlin so vehemently accused others of doing.[53] There is a distinction, he says, between 'political liberty' and 'economic liberty'. For me, however, this represents merely an excellent example of the kind of linguistic trick that will occupy a great deal of space in this book. As Berlin himself so eloquently put it, "liberty is liberty, not equality or fairness or justice or culture, or human happiness or a quiet conscience."[54] It can be added that liberty

---

[49] This feels like a slightly too rigid description of everyday human action and choice, as, of course, does much decision theory, but I don't think that this affects the overall point here.
[50] Berlin 2002a, p. 45.
[51] Berlin 2002a, p. 46 (my italics). See also Berlin 2002b, p. 172.
[52] Berlin 2002b, p. 169.
[53] This "sleight of hand" – what Berlin calls 'positive liberty' – is discussed below.
[54] Berlin 2002b, p. 172.

is liberty, not economic liberty, political liberty, circumstantial liberty, or anything else, just liberty.[55] The extent to which I am free is the extent of the number of choices and opportunities that are genuinely available and open to me, the size of the area in which I am left free to act, what I *can*, and am able to do, the doing of good in my own way.[56]

As I have said, liberty is a concept of degree[57] and to add the word 'political' to the front of it, is to do exactly what Berlin claims his opponents (who endorse economic 'slavery') are doing, namely adhering to a certain kind of subjectively-held theory,[58] that the only losses of freedom which are unacceptable, that matter morally speaking, or even, can be genuinely counted as losses of freedom, are those counted under the umbrella of the basic liberal rights. What Berlin (together with many others) adds to this story, is a theory of coercion. As he says, "coercion implies the deliberate interference of other human beings within the area in which I could otherwise act. You lack political liberty or freedom only if you are prevented from attaining a goal by human beings."[59]

Yet, as readers may already have realised, this account of coercion is confused. For Berlin had already claimed, in the passage I quoted earlier, that what matters is alterable human practices, deliberate or otherwise. Huge controversies begin to abound. Not only, as Berlin himself clearly realised,[60] are there few (if any) human actions which do not affect the liberty of other human beings, there will be equally few human practices which are not, in one sense or another, alterable.[61] Now, I do not wish to deny that these are key issues in any account of liberty, but they come later. We may not be able to do any better in terms of individual liberty, in any sustainable way, than under the alterable human practices we currently inhabit, but this is

---

[55] And, indeed, as I go on to discuss, the semantics of this are very important. See below.
[56] To paraphrase Mill 1991, pp. 16–17. Also, Berlin 2002b, p. 174.
[57] To put it another way. If I am able to afford certain things my neighbour cannot (if say, I can afford a sailing boat) then my degree of freedom, my area of free choice, is greater than hers, at least in certain ways (which do not, in other words, identify objects themselves with freedom, *per se*).
[58] Berlin 2002b, p. 170.
[59] Berlin 2002b, p. 169.
[60] See Berlin 2002b, p. 201.
[61] As is discussed in much greater detail below.

a separate matter which side-steps, by a 'sleight of hand', the central issue. We have already travelled quite some distance from the naked (as it were) concept of freedom and into deep and lengthy controversies which, at this stage, should not belong.

Not for one moment, I should point out, am I accusing Berlin of inhumanity or ignorance of the plight of those in poverty who suffer debilitating conditions – he was surely right to feel indignant towards those who did accuse him in such a way,[62] and anyone who has closely read 'Two Concepts of Liberty' will immediately see why. My point is the same as Berlin's.

Liberty is liberty. Liberty is liberty and nothing else, and if certain aspects of this concept are downgraded, disregarded or misunderstood, if certain implications of it are lost, then the concept itself is likely to be downgraded. Is it 'liberty' that is valuable or just (so-called) political liberty, and 'political liberty' masquerading, semantically, as 'liberty'? Does an absence of genuine choice suddenly stop mattering if the constraint is non-human, or if it is only caused by 'economic slavery' or by 'conditions'?[63] If 'liberty' can be applied to those who do suffer from abject poverty (because, for example, it is claimed that they are nominally protected by certain basic 'rights') and are simply unable to make any use of the choices and opportunities that are, theoretically, available to them,[64] this is to describe them and the society in which they live, in an impoverished and ultimately misleading way. It also, and much more importantly, may have the concomitant effect of placing them further down

---

[62] See Berlin 2002a, p. 38.
[63] See below on this point. It is clear that there are a number of controversies here, including (perhaps especially), what is to count as human constraint? It is arguments like this which take us away from the concept of liberty itself and on to different ground, including theories of coercion and restraint. But it seems to me that we will not get very far into the enterprise announced by those fundamental questions of political philosophy if we get sidetracked. It might be deeply inconvenient to start from the beginning with 'liberty' and liberty period (detached from any subjective theory of coercion or restraint), but if it is 'liberty' we are concerned with (as a good for human beings) there is no way round that. What we can *do* about the various degrees of unfreedom, or of unequal freedom (and, therefore, what is to count as a (so-called) unjustifiable restriction of freedom) comes at the next stage in the process.
[64] A few examples are given below, pp. 111–112. However, these can clearly never be anything other than a brief illustration of all the many forms of loss of freedom faced by human beings today.

the list of those in need of help and take them further out of the minds of the reformers.[65]

Belief that the unfortunate and underprivileged do in fact possess 'liberty' has a necessary effect on our moral thinking and moral ordering. Therefore, it is certainly true that this is not merely a pedantic distinction. The words 'free society' are particularly prone to misuse in this regard. Britain is frequently described as a 'free society' (and its inhabitants as enjoying 'liberty'[66]) for example, but free for whom, and liberty of what kind and to what degree? There might be good reasons and good evidence for believing this claim (at least relatively so) and I shall come back to this,[67] but what about Britain's homeless? What about those whose daily lives are beset by the lack of opportunities and choice engendered through conditions of poverty, prejudice, disempowerment, deprivation and isolation?[68]

There is a further point more important still than the previous two. If, as I have discussed, liberty is of fundamental importance to human beings, and if, to (arbitrarily for the moment) bring in another concept, all human beings are by virtue of the humanity into which they are born, 'equal', then why do we condone and allow conditions (across the globe, in the cosmopolitan sense, and within our own 'affluent' countries, in a more limited sense) of not only greatly unequal freedom, but even abject slavery[69] and further, the final destruction of human freedom resulting from loss of life?[70] We are all promised 'equal liberty',[71] but if that equal liberty means solely an equality of the basic liberal rights and freedoms (important as these so clearly are), that suggests a much reduced amount of equal freedom than might be the case

---

[65] I return to this later, pp. 111 ff below.
[66] A classic illustration of this by the current Prime Minister, can be found in Brown 2007.
[67] See p. 80. below.
[68] For an excellent illustration of this problem, in American inner cities, see Wilson 1996, pp. 51–86.
[69] There are reliably estimated to be well over 20 million people currently held in actual physical servitude across the globe, no different to the slaves of ancient Greece and Rome and the antebellum American South. See Bales 1999. Some are much closer to us than we might think. It is thought that there could be as many as 5000 slaves in Paris alone.
[70] Thomas Pogge, in an excellent book, says that around 50,000 people die every day from preventable causes. Pogge 2002, p. 2.
[71] See below, pp. 110 ff.

were the understanding of the word freedom to be expanded, if for example, Berlin's arbitrary distinction,[72] were rejected. What we mean by our use of the word 'liberty' is of vital importance (especially when our other normative concepts come into the picture), since what we *mean* by 'liberty' then comes to mean, in turn, what we are entitled to from liberty (as it were). I shall be shortly returning to these issues.

One important corollary of what I am saying here is that there does not need to be a form of human coercion, of "deliberate interference" on the part of other human beings, for there to be a loss, or a restriction, of freedom. Nor, further, that only such a situation constitutes a truly unacceptable loss of liberty. Remember, I am saying that, if we are investigating how much 'liberty' (nothing else, no other concept) can be enjoyed by human beings living at a particular moment in human society over time, we are talking purely about liberty and nothing else. We will not get very far with this enterprise if we start dressing up the concept of freedom in subjective (and arguably arbitrary, but certainly controversial) theories of constraint, oppression and coercion. Still, regardless of all this, liberty is liberty and nothing else – as Berlin is himself at pains to remind us. This is not to say that coercion (or any other theory) is not important, it clearly is, but an absence of human coercion (or an absence of 'arbitrary' human coercion, or whatever theory of coercion a given writer happens to hold dear[73]) is not the same as liberty, pure and simple.

For instance, although I don't think it makes sense for a human being to say that they have been deprived of freedom because they cannot swim like a dolphin, or fly like an eagle, or sting like a wasp,[74] I think it makes profound sense for a disabled person, for example, to say that they lack certain freedoms because they lack the choices we take as basic to

---

[72] Between 'freedom' and the 'conditions for its exercise'. However, this is slightly unfair to Berlin as he is far from being the only one to adhere to this distinction. See, for example, p. 115 below.

[73] See, for example, Pettit 2007, pp. 717–718.

[74] Not to say that you couldn't make yourself understood by speaking in this way, especially if you were a poet. Still the point remains, these attributes or abilities are non-human. At least for the moment, though there is clearly a strange (perhaps bizarre) sense in which this *could* possibly change and the dimensions of human freedom will have to be rewritten. Freedom evolves, just like humans, just like human society and just like language.

human life and, what is more, which could be returned to them if the alterable human world were changed in certain ways. If, that is, the world were adapted better so that people with disabilities could have more choice and therefore, more freedom in their lives. Things *could* be different,[75] as the social model of disability has been vehemently and convincingly arguing over the last few decades. The fact that I, a double amputee, cannot swim in my local pool because it lacks the equipment and/or the personnel to allow me to safely do so, whilst my friend, who has the same condition, but who lives in a city with a pool with better facilities can, suggests that the lack of choice is not related to my physical condition, at least not solely. Again, there are clearly 'alterable human practices' at play here.

Now Berlin says that "if my poverty were a kind of disease which prevented me from buying bread or paying for the journey round the world or getting my case heard, as lameness prevents me from running, this inability would not naturally be described as a lack of freedom, least of all political freedom."[76] Berlin may *possibly* be right that 'lameness preventing me from running' does not count as an absence of (what he calls) political freedom, according to his own subjective theory of what that means (i.e. where the coercion is human and deliberate[77]), but in terms of freedom pure and simple, his claim clearly will not do.

---

[75] See my conclusion below on this last point.
[76] Berlin 2002b, p. 170.
[77] However, note that my example above somewhat contradicts this, at least in certain circumstances related to physical disability. Further of course, as human moral evolution (to which I shall return) slowly advances, we are, as a society, belatedly understanding more and more the implications of 'equal human rights' in relation to disabled people (as well as other groups). The language of 'equal opportunities' here raises interesting questions about how the alterable shape of the world constrains disabled people. Since we could do something about this, but choose not to, this could, without much controversy to my mind, count as deliberate coercion on the part of other human beings. Apathy is a human action, a deed, too. Note, again, however, we have been sidetracked (by a theory of coercion or restraint), from a key unfreedom which could be altered regardless of who, or what, does the constraining.

The reason for this is that Berlin takes his task (partly) to be defining freedom in the 'normal' sense of the word.[78] Imagine you had just met a wheelchair-bound person on a road, following a revolution in a totalitarian state which prevented people from running, whose government had been overturned, and you said to her 'you are free to run!' Further, as Oscar Pistorius has been showing on the world stage, it is possible for double amputees to run, and to run very fast. The tools are there, for some at least. What matters, in terms of liberty, is that the choice is denied to those who don't have access to such tools and what matters, at the next stage in the process,[79] is why they don't have access to them, whether that lack of access is acceptable and, if so, on what grounds, or, if not, what can be done about it? Equality, at this stage, will begin to prove a heavy load to bare, as we shall see.

Freedom and the Conditions for its Exercise

Now, imagine two societies. One is governed by a dictator who allows none of her citizens to have an education for fear that they would learn the ways and means of destroying her rule. None of her citizens, except for a few close family members, are free to have an education. Not only is their freedom constrained by fear of her secret police, as well as her strong central bureaucratic infrastructure, but even some, or most, of the essential means of education (schools, books and so on) have been destroyed.

The second society is a liberal democracy ruled by an everyday centre-right representative party. This government does not prevent any of its citizens from having an education, indeed it has laws which require all to have an education up to a certain age (16, say).[80] However, after this certain age, fees are charged at a reasonably high rate for education to continue and

---

[78] E.g. Berlin, 2002a, p. 48; 2002b, p. 169.
[79] Edge (Forthcoming C).
[80] Note the interesting paradox here. The children of the dictator's nation are forced into not having an education, whilst the children of the liberal nation are forced into having an education (up to a certain age). So, perhaps, the degree of unfreedom (or so it could be argued, at least) is not all that different between them. Despite this, it is clear which one we look on more positively and this illustrates nicely (what I never mean to deny) that other values can surpass liberty in certain moral questions.

this cuts off a certain percentage of the population from receiving this further education.[81] To these people, the opportunity to have a further education, the freedom to do so, is not available. They are barely in a better position than the citizens of the dictator, who are forced to work in a certain job, without any access to education at all. If more information is given and this society resembles a modern capitalist liberal democracy, certainly more degrees of liberty are available to the poor and underprivileged of this state than the citizens living under the dictator. They should have access to free libraries, to systems of adult education as their lives progress, as well as to books and the Internet (though, again, this will be by degree), but it remains a simple fact that they are not free to access or use, what, under the conditions of this society (which again, *could* be changed, they are not a part of the natural, 'factual', makeup of things), they cannot afford to do.[82] They are prevented from doing (in Berlin's terms) 'what they could otherwise do'.[83]

In comparison, the second society fares very well (and this, as I shall discuss further, is an important point). A large percentage of the population, even 60%, has free, open and easy access to basic and higher education, and the background structure of this affluent society has resulted in the creation of further educational mechanisms. Yet it is undeniable that

---

[81] Some will object that, if, say, I am talking about contemporary Britain, then this example is too simplistic. Through, they might say, the capitalist infrastructure (student loans etc.), and certain governmental incentives (grants etc.), money is available to all to help them with their studies. Students could also work to support themselves during their studies. To these objections I would counter: 1. The fear itself of the (in some cases vast) financial penalties facing students leaving university, who come from less privileged backgrounds, would itself be a huge deterrent. 2. This system might also, in some cases, be too reliant on the capitalist infrastructure (such as the availability of work, for example). 3. Arguably most importantly, such an objection could not itself ignore the large inequalities in (to borrow Rawls' term) the basic structure of society in relation to education. It is a simple fact that children from poorer, more deprived neighbourhoods, especially those where violent crime is a major problem, find it harder to access education, not least because of the great inequality in resources between schools. This is not to say that children from less privileged backgrounds can never reach higher education (I have been fortunate enough to teach them), but this is hardly the point.

[82] Consider this in relation to pp. 26–30 below.

[83] See p. 108 below. It is after all the laws of society, relating to pay, purchase and exchange (in this case), which ultimately prevent me. I am naturally forbidden *by law* from taking what I cannot afford to buy.

certain important freedoms remain denied to a large number because of the makeup of that society, and further, this society is an affluent one. In less fortunate parts of the world (with which I am equally, if not more, concerned), millions of children are denied access to basic education because they are forced to work alongside, or separate from, their parents, so that the family can survive. Education is a good example to use, because it is (or can be) an important ingredient of human liberty,[84] but the point could be made just as well by discussing other choices, opportunities and objects which are denied to millions of human beings because they simply cannot afford and are, therefore, not able, to access them. They are not part of their 'choice range'.

To help illustrate my argument let me try to provide (that dreaded term) 'a snapshot of life'. Lionel X and Lionel Y both live in a Northern Town in England. Both are able bodied and can play football and, since they live in Britain, they are not prevented by the coercive laws of their society from playing football (unlike Afghani females under the Taliban[85]). Lionel X and Lionel Y also don't feel that it is a restriction on their freedom (they are both pretty genial, uncontroversial, fellows) that they cannot play football with the same degree of skill as their Argentinean namesake Lionel Messi.[86] They don't have the same degree of freedom concerning football matters as Messi (though we can expect that their other 'natural abilities' offer them, or correctly, *could* offer them,[87] opportunities Messi could not make use of). In other words, they don't have the (potential

---

[84] Cf. pp. 95–96 below.
[85] This also points to the fact that freedom can often be gender specific and, naturally, that it is women, as opposed to men, who have suffered most, historically speaking, from this. Although this is – once again – largely a matter for the next stage of the process, it must still be noted here how the difference in masculine and feminine biology and physiology does have an impact, and a massive one at that, on free choice. This point is particularly well made by Hirschmann 2002.
[86] However, there *could* be controversies here too. Lionel X could actually have gone on to play professional football (he had the innate ability to do so), but his parents could not afford the proper equipment and club fees for training when he was younger and he gave up.
[87] See n. 86 above. Once again, there are significant controversies here as to how social conditions enable us to make the best of our selves according to our 'natural abilities'. It is just that, at this stage, since I am dealing with liberty and nothing else, it is better to avoid them. Cf. Berlin 2002b, p. 170.

perhaps) choice to play for Barcelona, Manchester United or the LA Galaxy, or Hearts of Oak, or even the semi-professional team in the town in which they live (Messi could, theoretically, choose to play for that team). However, they are still able to play football. Whereas Messi's abilities give him the choice to play football as a profession, theirs don't. They are free to try to play professional football but, as things stand, they are not likely to get very far.

Lionel X and Lionel Y have both arranged to play football on a Saturday in December. Lionel Y's partner then asks him, the day after he has made this arrangement, if he would like to go to watch the local football team's league match which just happens to be taking place at the same time Lionel Y has arranged to play football. Lionel Y, therefore, finds himself faced with a choice-dilemma. Lionel X's partner also had the same thought about going to see the local football team but didn't express it because he knew that the two of them could not both afford to buy a ticket. No money remains in their bank accounts after basic essentials, including bills, have been taken care of, and Lionel X and his partner have always resolved never to go into debt because they understand that this will greatly affect their freedom of choice in the future, owing to the fact that they do not bring in large salaries. Lionel X and his partner also live in a deprived, disadvantaged, part of town because that is the only area they can afford the rent, whereas Lionel Y and his partner rent a house in a more affluent area with more amenities. This has, as I have hinted at, also affected their choices and opportunities (and therefore their freedom) throughout life, but to steer clear of controversy, I won't discuss this further here.[88]

Now, on the Friday night before Lionel X and Lionel Y's scheduled games of football, it snows heavily. Both parks where the two Lionels were scheduled to play, in their respective parts of town, are completely carpeted in snow. Fortunately for

---

[88] Let's say also, for the moment, that Lionel X's upbringing affected his freedom in other ways. He was, for instance, a young carer for his sick father because the family could not afford extra support. Although happy to do this, he still resented the extra choices and opportunities some of his wealthier friends at school had. This also affected his schoolwork and he dropped out at 16. Of course, there is (or could be) a lot more to Lionel X's story, but I'll leave it there for the moment. Cf. n. 86 above.

Lionel Y, his club could afford a part-time groundsman and a state-of-the-art snow clearing machine, so the groundsman clears the snow early on the Saturday. Unfortunately for Lionel X, his club could not afford this machine (or a groundsman) and his friends are forced to cancel the game as the snow is too thick for them to clear themselves. For the record, Lionel Y decides to go and watch the match rather than play with his friends.

This might be a pithy example and it deals with absolute choices in a slightly unnatural way, but still it could hardly be denied that the stories of Lionel X and Lionel Y do reflect reality in a number of important ways.

It should be uncontroversial that Lionel Y possesses greater choice and, therefore, greater freedom under Berlin's own analysis.[89] Yet those of us who make this claim are told that we have made a 'mistake', are riddled with confusions, or have made a 'philosophical error' because, among other things, there is no human coercion here,[90] no explicit, no 'arbitrary' or deliberate human coercion. Yet Lionel X still lacks certain choices, certain opportunities, which Lionel Y does not (regardless of who or what denies him them). Therefore, I doubt that the error or the confusion (if there is one) is mine. Whether Lionel X's loss if liberty is unacceptable and, just as importantly, whether something can legitimately be done about it,[91] his loss of liberty is still a loss of liberty. Whether I have been killed by a car accident, by a freak flood, or murdered by a rival, I am no less dead. Responsibility is clearly an issue above this (so to speak), a matter for another time or place.

What we can, and what we should (if anything) do about Lionel X's loss of liberty – and why – comes at the next stage of the process when we are actually dealing, above the groundwork as it were, with those fundamental questions of political philosophy. However, it will not do to duck the issue by suggesting that Lionel X somehow has the same degree of freedom as Lionel Y. He doesn't, unless you want to deny that choice or opportunity is connected to freedom,[92] or perhaps to

---

[89] See the quote on p. 17 above.
[90] See p. 115 below.
[91] See Edge (Forthcoming C).
[92] This is not to say that greater choice always equals greater *happiness* (Lionel Y's football team ends up losing and he spends the rest of the weekend

claim, that choice is, or becomes, unimportant when it is denied by non-human factors, but that, clearly, will not do either and for the same reasons. For instance, you could somehow try to claim that it would matter, in terms of 'freedom', if I am denied the choice to eat (or not to eat) by a dictator, or a judge, but that it would not matter, in terms of freedom, if I am denied that choice by 'economic forces' or 'the forces of circumstance', because there is no human constraint (perhaps only apathy or inaction) in the second case. But that is paradoxical and still the fundamental problem would remain, i.e. trying to deny that choice is linked to freedom (regardless of who or what constrains that choice). And here, the choice is the most fundamental of all – the choice to eat or refrain from eating – on which all future individual liberty is based.

If I cannot get to the stadium to watch my team play football, whether I am prevented by the iron hand of a dictator, a snowstorm which has blocked the road from my house, a strike on the buses, or the price of the ticket, I am not free to go. If we are concerned with human freedom, and freedom only, it does not matter whether I am coerced or prevented, or forced against my will, by a lack of 'political liberty', 'economic liberty', or 'circumstantial liberty', what matters, if we are to value and treat liberty as liberty, is that I lack the opportunity to go. The choice is denied me. To be sure, interlinked here are many vital questions related to moral and political philosophy, including those two central questions of political philosophy I began with. What I am arguing here is that before we can even hope to attempt a beginning of an answer to those (and other) questions, we must first recognise, and treat, liberty as liberty, and a loss of liberty as a loss of liberty and not undermine and downgrade its meaning and potential by dressing it up in a conceptual language which does not (at this stage at least) belong.

First Final Thoughts

Freedom is freedom, not equality, not justice, not happiness, not a quiet conscience, not an education, not peace. These

---

wishing he had played football himself instead), but that is, again, off the point and also not generally speaking – how human life is lived and how human decisions are made otherwise, indeed, freedom and choice would not be valuable or, at least, not as valuable.

are Berlin's (paraphrased) words, not mine. What I have been arguing in the preceding pages is that if we are to have any hope of even attempting to discover how much freedom each of us is able to enjoy in a sustainable human environment ,then we must begin with freedom itself, detached from all the subjective epistemological and theoretical baggage it tends to carry.

One of the reasons for this is simply, as I have been keen to point out, that human freedom is restricted by factors other than 'deliberate human interference', regardless of what you might happen to mean by that controversial phrase. The doors which are theoretically open to us, according to those natural abilities we possess, and are able to develop through time,[93] are closed, shut, or firmly concreted over, by factors other than deliberate human interference. If we want to attempt an answer to the question we began with, we must begin at a point before theories of (what constitutes) deliberate human interference (and other theories and beliefs) even enter the equation.

Freedom is about the world, the environment we live in and our surroundings, possibly even as much as it is about other human beings. And here, perhaps, Berlin's awkward phrase 'alterable human practices' comes in. The obvious problem is that there an awfully large number of alterable human practices, but before we give up on the phrase entirely, it certainly does point to something useful, if also challenging.

What is needed is an account – or in the theory I am outlining here, competing accounts – of how different human practices promote individual freedom and the reasons for that. This is precisely what I will attempt to do myself in part two of this project. Clearly, this is a complex task, but if we value human liberty and wish to get the best from it, there is no way around that, or so I have been arguing.

We may not be able to do better (either in terms of the amount of freedom each of us has and/or the degree of equality in which we possess it), though that, given the levels of tragedy that currently swamp human lives across the globe today, is

---

[93] Which development, is equally dependent on the availability or otherwise of open doors. Further, as I have suggested, the phrase 'natural abilities' raises issues of its own. See Edge (Forthcoming D).

a highly depressing thought and is one I do not share.[94] In other words, one thing these competing accounts of freedom will have to satisfy is a slightly amended version of Rawls' difference principle.[95] This is the idea that, if we are to justify inequalities (in freedom in my case), then those inequalities must be to the benefit of the worse off. This idea is not without its controversies – it is still open to you to argue that, regardless of the fact that the worse off will still be better off under the unequal system, inequality is still morally unjustified because of the equal status all human beings have (and I have some sympathy with this argument), it does provide a useful starting place to think about the question and certainly provides one of the criteria for judgement. One of the things that I am arguing here, is that the 'worse off' are likely to be better off if they are given the opportunity to decide this for themselves, rather than the matter being judged on some subjective account of human rationality and interest, more on which in a moment.

As someone once succinctly, and very helpfully put it to me, the key is to maintain diversity whilst securing equality.[96] How can opportunities, bundles of individual liberty, be equalised, or at least more equalised? What therefore is needed is an account of how human labour, and the kind of society built around and by it, will support individual human liberty according to the resources available to us. How, essentially, human beings, engaged in cooperation together, will be able to sustain whatever degree of equal liberty a given account calls for. I give a few indications below of the kind of increases in, both, degrees of individual human freedom, and, with that, the degree to which that increased freedom could be enjoyed equally by human beings, below, but the full account must wait until the second part of the project.

This is why I have argued that we must begin with freedom itself, and detach the concept from the modern theories and subjective beliefs, thoughts and prejudices which shroud it. My own account in part two will be no less subjective, but,

---
[94] As will be evidenced by Edge (Forthcoming C).
[95] See, for example, Rawls 1996, pp. 6 ff.; Rawls 1999a, pp. 65–70; Rawls 2001, § 18, pp. 61–66.
[96] I would like to thank Kostas Vlassopoulos for this typically helpful summation. I do not wish to imply that he will agree with what I take to be its consequences.

ultimately, that is unavoidable[97] but, as I say, must come later in the process. The consequences of taking a starting point elsewhere are, as I have argued, that freedom itself and all the many and tragic ways human freedom can be hindered, lessened and annihilated, are likely to be forgotten in favour of some subjective account of it. There is also however, a further consequence which I now wish to turn to, and while it is one identified by liberal writers, we might wonder whether they have always situated it in the right place.

---

[97] See pp. 98–107 below.

Chapter Two
The Problem of Positive Liberty

Positive and Negative Freedom

When Sir Isaiah Berlin delivered his famous address on freedom in 1958, he made an equally famous distinction between positive and negative freedom, which has retained a great deal of influence on the literature ever since. Although there are problems with his argument,[98] the consequences Berlin believed to emanate from doctrines of positive freedom had a huge influence on his analysis and he identified those consequences as the path to tyranny, despotism and totalitarianism. In this chapter, I will discuss those consequences in greater depth, since, in the theory I am constructing here, an answer to the problem of positive freedom is key, for reasons which will shortly become clear. I have intimated throughout that the ones who should be providing the answer to those fundamental questions I began with are, simply, each of us together, the collective people. It is when we get on to the issue of positive freedom that further reasons for this become clear and they are reasons and consequences that would, in all probability, be quite surprising to Berlin, as he tended to see these kind of democratic conclusions as the epitome of positive liberty doctrines leading to totalitarianism and tyranny.[99] But first things first.

In Berlin's analysis, on the other side to positive freedom – to which I shall shortly return – stands negative liberty. Negative liberty is the straightforward idea that I have been discussing in the preceding pages. It is simply, "the area within which a man can act unobstructed by others."[100] "If I

---
[98] Discussed in greater detail in Edge (Forthcoming B).
[99] See, especially, Berlin 2002b, pp. 208–212.
[100] Berlin 2002b, p. 169.

am prevented by others from doing what I could otherwise do," Berlin continues, "I am to that degree unfree."[101] Or, as I have argued (*contra* Berlin), negative liberty is simply the area within which a human can act unobstructed (regardless of who, or what, might be doing the obstructing and why). My area of negative liberty, in other words, according to the analysis in the preceding pages, is the area of free movement left to me by the society in which I live, its laws and morality, as well as its level of technological development and its economic and social systems (together with a number of other things). All these combine and dictate the size of the area in which I am (in real everyday life) left free to go my own way and am left to do my own thing and am free to make the choices I choose.

Positive liberty, Berlin claims, is a different animal entirely. It is the doctrine of liberation by reason, or self-mastery, or, in notably Platonic terms, of the conquest of the lower part of the human soul (spirit/psyche/personality) by the higher. In other words, rather than leaving the choice to me as to how I am to make use of my liberty, the positive doctrine of liberation by reason sees freedom in individuals acting a certain way, or in following a particular 'true' path which will lead to (true) liberty.[102] Berlin finds this doctrine in the work of such thinkers as Rousseau, Kant, Fichte and even his fellow liberal T.H. Green.[103]

Now, as Quentin Skinner has correctly pointed out, Berlin's argument has a number of false starts. Berlin first tries to link the doctrine of positive liberty to the idea of being one's own master.[104] But, as Skinner also argues, if I am not my own master, if I am under the control of others, if I am not free to choose the way I am to go, then I would appear to be unfree in the simple negative sense.[105]

Berlin links the idea of negative liberty to the question 'how far am I governed?' and he links the idea of positive liberty to the question 'who governs me?' and he sees a clear

---
[101] Ibid.
[102] See Berlin 2002b, pp. 178-181 and ff.
[103] Cf. Berlin 2002d.
[104] Berlin 2002b, p. 178.
[105] See Skinner 2001, pp. 238-239.

distinction between them.[106] He has a point. These two are, to some degree, logically distinct. Clearly, as Berlin realised, I could choose, if I so desired, to impose a stricter form of life or control, over myself, if I did 'govern myself', if I was completely autonomous.[107] In doing so, I would be, *de facto*, shrinking my area of negative liberty to do what I want, go where I want and say what I want. However, Berlin already has a problem here. As I said earlier, Berlin's discussion of negative liberty includes the idea that this 'negative' realm of mine, free from interference and coercion by others, gives me the room to 'go my own way' and 'do my own thing' and pursue my own conception of the good life. He also quotes Mill approvingly to this effect.[108]

Imagine the following situation.[109] The peoples of the world, fed up with fighting one another, decide to construct a contract of peace. Traditional nation-states are abolished and an absolute guarantee (for all time) of freedom of movement between the various territories is established and granted to all the inhabitants of the earth.[110] The peoples of the earth then set up a number of different polities, organised along the lines of what each conceives to be 'the good'. For example, let's say that there are Muslim polities for Shias and Sunnis, a Kurdistan, a polity for Sufis, one for doctrinal Catholics and for Protestants; a fully communist polity; a rural, vegetarian, Buddhist sanctuary; a liberal capitalist territory; a society of pure anarchism, a strict conservative society organised according to an entrenched and far-reaching moral code, and so on.

---

[106] See, for example, Berlin 2002b, p. 177.
[107] As some people, do, of course, who (for example) withdraw from society and from social relations and live a strict life in adherence to a certain moral code, as is the case in certain forms of aestheticism.
[108] See Berlin 2002b, p.174.
[109] I am not, I should point out, arguing on behalf of this situation and there are clearly many faults with the example (which is part of the reason I would not advocate it), but they do not touch the basic point.
[110] Note, here, how important freedom of movement is to freedom in general, though it is not generally included in most discussions of the 'basic liberties'. If I am (genuinely) free to move, then I can escape any form of coercion or unfreedom I so desire. Our societies seem to be getting worse and worse at granting freedom of movement, particularly for those who really need it – refugees and asylum seekers. This is discussed in full in part two.

Can those, in such a situation, who choose to live under the stricter polities (providing of course, that they do genuinely have the opportunity to choose to leave them at any time), which offer less negative liberty (in Berlin's sense) to their inhabitants really be designated unfree? Plato's Socrates recognised this long ago in the *Krito*. If Berlin did want to argue this (and I don't think he necessarily would), he would, I think, be reduced to arguing on psychological grounds – something to the effect that those who rejected the liberal polity and therefore, a basic degree of 'liberal negative liberty' had been brainwashed, induced, misled or duped. However, ironically, this would already begin to sound like something more sinister – on (what would be) Berlin's part – since it locates the psychological error, untruth, stupidity, or whatever, in those who are not able to see their own best interest, i.e. what is on offer in liberal polities[111], but this, as Berlin certainly and passionately realised, and as I will shortly come on to discuss, has highly problematic consequences of its own.

Are those who choose to live in the more 'repressive', conservative, polities still not fulfilling the criterion of 'doing their own good in their own way'? They have chosen freely from any number of conflicting alternatives and could leave at any time. Who is Berlin (or any other liberal) to tell them they are unfree and that, only by removing themselves to the liberal polity could they hope to be free? What is it that makes them any less free in the simple negative sense? Of course, there *is* a problem with what is to constitute a free choice here, and why,[112] but it clearly will not do for liberals to say that they, and only they, are in possession of the correct form of free thought, which has given them the foresight to choose liberalism, therein locating correct human psychology, or rationality, or choice, decision or whatever with liberalism. This is paradoxical and, as we shall see shortly, will not do, and it won't do for Berlin as much as it won't do for me.

It is when Berlin gets on to the arguments he perceives as being behind the idea of 'being one's own master' that he does have something very important – and very unsettling

---

[111] But what would the communists say to the liberals?
[112] See Edge (Forthcoming D).

– to say. Related to this idea of 'being one's own master', Berlin says, is the doctrine of the two selves.[113] This theory, familiar to readers of Plato (among others), suggests that, as a human being, I possess two selves, a lower and a higher. The lower self is traditionally related to the base and vulgar passions, lower desires and hungers, whereas the higher self is commonly linked to rationality or reason. Only when, the argument runs, my higher self has control of my lower, can I be said to be truly free and to enjoy 'liberty'.

Berlin finds a sinister twist to this story. If I have attained this higher state of being for myself, 'true liberty', proper rationality, the one 'true' path, then, as I look down upon my poor fellow human beings, still struggling to master the raging passions, desires and hungers of their lower selves, am I not justified in using all the corrective and coercive force at my disposal to put them on the correct path? If they cannot see it for themselves, if they are unable to attain true liberty by their own efforts, it will clearly be better for them if I help to bring them up towards the light, even if I have to use coercion to do so.[114] "This", as Berlin explains, "renders it easy for me to conceive of myself as coercing others for their own sake, in their, not my, interest. I am then claiming that I know what they truly need better than they know it themselves."[115]

> This monstrous impersonation, [Berlin goes on], which consists in equating what X would choose if he were something he is not, or at least not yet, with what X actually seeks and chooses, is at the heart of all political theories of self-realisation. It is one thing to say that I may be coerced for my own good, which I am too blind to see: this may, on occasion, be for my benefit; indeed it may enlarge the scope for my liberty. It is another to say that if it is my good, then I am not being coerced, for I have willed it, whether I know this or not, and am free (or 'truly' free) even while my poor earthly body and foolish mind bitterly reject it, and struggle with the greatest desperation against those who seek, however benevolently, to impose it.[116]

---

[113] It is important to point out that a doctrine of the two selves does not necessarily lead to totalitarianism and tyranny. See Edge (Forthcoming B).
[114] This is exactly the sort of reasoning used in Heidegger 2002, part 1, pp. 1–106.
[115] Berlin 2002b, p. 179, and see ff.
[116] Berlin 2002b, pp. 180–181.

Pandora's Box

There are a few further problems with Berlin's analysis. For one thing, he is light (in 'Two Concepts of Liberty', at least) on quotations to support the link between the doctrine of positive liberty and various totalitarian and monstrous movements across the globe.[117] This is not to deny the link,[118] but some more work might usefully be done on how great a historical link there actually is. Secondly, and in relation to this, we must not assume that it is only the concept of liberty that can be manipulated in this way, a point which I feel has not received the attention it deserves. The word 'liberty' could easily be substituted for 'happiness' or 'peace' in such arguments and the effects of them would remain much the same. In other words, that true happiness, or true peace, or the true state of some other concept, can only be found in mastering the self to follow a particular kind of regime or path or truth, or, even, in mastering the (so-called) lower hungers, desires and passions.

The key to this – as Berlin pointed out – is that the inherent truth (or way of being) of whatever concept it is you happen to be concerned with, whether peace, happiness, liberty or any other concept, becomes linked with your own subjective interpretation, or version, of it. What matters (and here the fact that Berlin was a little light on concrete doctrinal links is certainly significant) is how, historically speaking, movements, parties, groups and individuals have managed to use this kind of language and with what effect. There can be little doubt that such language is certainly pernicious, but in order for it to have a truly pernicious effect, those who preach it must possess the tools to cause other human beings to accept it as true, or at the very least, to turn a blind eye to aspects of discomfort contained in the analysis or doctrine.

This is to open Pandora's box, and to open it wide. What does make human beings susceptible to such language and its effects? To this question, there are almost as many answers as there are thinking human beings on the planet (thinking, it is worth pointing out, at a particular place, and a particular

---

[117] See, for example, Fontana 1988, p. 26.
[118] See, for example, Heidegger 1993, a classic illustration of this kind of doctrine from within Nazi Germany.

The Problem of Positive Liberty

moment of historical time). We have our beliefs, fears, neuroses, worries, stresses, prejudices (and various other things), all historically accumulated in our minds over time, and these can be (and have been) readily played on by various groups and individuals looking to exploit our shortcomings. An idea (if it in fact existed[119]) like 'true German liberty (happiness, peace, being, or whatever) can only be accomplished once the 'lower self' of German society, the Jews, is completely extinguished' would, itself, have played on a number of other (probably widely-held) beliefs and, of course, prejudices about both German and Jewish society, a number of them economic in character. Right-wing organisations and movements have proved (and are still proving) adept at making use out of people's fears for political purposes.

Fear (of whatever kind) is a notable barrier to free thought and free action because it closes the mind off from certain choices which it believes – for whatever reason – to be undesirable, irrational and frightening, but I shall come back to this. Marx once wrote to Arnold Ruge, "for our part it is our task to drag the old world into the full light of day and to give positive shape to the new one. The more time history allows thinking mankind to reflect and suffering mankind to collect its strength the more perfect will be the fruit which the present now bears within its womb."[120] It sounds remarkably simple, in theory, to 'lift the old world into the full light of day' and many have, of course, attempted to do so yet, in practice, the attempt continues to prove elusive. The accumulated collection of thoughts, beliefs, neuroses, fears and prejudices that are materialised in the individuals living in a given society, at a given moment of historical time, prove hard nuts to crack. Part of the answer to this – increasing our amount of (what might be termed) 'epistemological freedom'[121] – is discussed in chapter three, but there is another step in the argument to be considered first.

---

[119] I am using this solely as an example, but I have little doubt that this kind of thinking certainly existed in Nazi Germany. Indeed, it would have had to have done for the kind of mass evil which occurred under the Nazis to have been practised in the first place. What we cannot record, of course, is how widely, and how deeply, such claims were believed.
[120] Marx 1975d, p. 206.
[121] What I mean by this is made much clearer below. See especially, pp. 94 ff below.

Positive Liberty and Democracy

Berlin argued for a distinction between those two questions ('how far am I governed?' and 'by whom am I governed?') but he failed to ask a further one which points to an interesting problem about the relationship between those first two questions. It is 'why am I governed?'

Although I do not wish to commit the cardinal sin of reducing the entire history of political thought to a pithy sentence, the answer to this has typically (though I do not – quite – say universally) been that I, as a member of that collective entity, 'the people', have to be governed because I am incapable of doing it myself.[122] It has traditionally been argued that I am incapable of governing myself and would do great damage, both to myself and my individual liberty (together with that of my fellow citizens), if I tried. It is, therefore, better for me to submit to the benevolent care of the most knowledgeable, or most wise, members of my community because I do not possess the requisite skills, rationality, knowledge or ability to do this myself. The next step has been to equate this situation with 'freedom'. Far from being considered as a form of coercion, or oppression, this is what is thought, in the modern world, to be 'liberty', i.e. living under a government run by a succession of our representatives who protect our rights and liberties and take on the task of governing in our stead.

By failing to ask this question ('why am I governed?'), I will here suggest, Berlin overlooked a problem regarding the relationship between his versions of positive and negative liberty, as well as a link between positive liberty arguments and non-participatory forms of government.[123]

The alarm bells should begin to ring when it is considered that (what Berlin depicts as) the positive conception of liberty became prominent (in Plato) as a response, in Classical Greece, to the democratic idea of liberty I have attempted to excavate elsewhere.[124] What so irked Plato (and others) about

---

[122] See Edge 2009 and (Forthcoming A) on this point. See also Roberts 1994 for a comprehensive survey of anti-democratic thought throughout the ages.
[123] The following argument is a (highly) condensed version of Edge (Forthcoming A).
[124] See Edge 2009 and (Forthcoming A).

democracy, was that it gave that part of society which was so overcome by the teeming passions and hungers of its lower self (i.e., the masses, the people, the so called lower classes), political rights, which he (and others) simply felt they were not entitled to, precisely because they were ruled by their lower, and not by the reason and rationality of their higher, selves. In Greek anti-democratic thought (and in Plato in particular), society as a whole is construed as possessing two selves, and it was thought that the lower (the masses), who could barely distinguish what it was in their best interests to want, were better off without political rights and, therefore, without a share in governing the city. Government, it was held, should be left to those capable of it, those who had mastered their raging passions and desires, society's higher self.

It is more than a little ironic that this connection has been missed because of the constant association of positive liberty with participatory democracy when, in fact, participatory democracy was thought (in the Athenian conception of negative liberty I have discussed elsewhere), precisely, to be a refuge for the common people from the control and authority related to these (and similar) claims of 'self-mastery' and sobriety.

Significantly, the idea that society possessed a natural class, or hierarchy, who could better discern society's true interests than could society itself collected together for that purpose, was also popular among many defenders of representative government, when the theory began to emerge, first in the seventeenth century, then, later, at the time of the American and French Revolutions. Again, I will not be able to go into this in detail here,[125] but the *locus classicus* of such arguments is James Madison's analysis in the *Federalist* no.10. Here, Madison famously extolled the virtues of "republican" ("representative") government as opposed to "pure" democracy.

> The effect of the first difference [citizens elect representatives rather than forming the government themselves], is, on the one hand, to refine and enlarge the public view, by passing them through the medium of a chosen body of citizens, whose wisdom *may best discern the true interest of their country*, and

[125] For a full(er) survey see Edge (Forthcoming A).

whose patriotism and love of justice, will be least likely to sacrifice it to temporary or partial considerations. Under such a regulation it may well happen that the public voice pronounced by the representatives of the people, will be more consonant to the public good, than if pronounced by the people themselves convened for this purpose.[126]

Other views of representation in the *Federalist* are very similar.[127]

Indeed, similar views still exist today. For example, in his article, itself entitled "Representation *is* Democracy" (my italics), David Plotke provides a defence of representation and attacks participatory accounts of democracy as fundamentally incoherent.[128] "A political representative", Plotke states, "looks towards the preferences of those they represent, towards others' preferences and toward their own view of overall welfare. Political representatives recognise the existence of competing and general interests alongside those of their constituents. *And they consider whether their constituents' choices are the best way to get what those constituents want.*"[129] Here, again, we have the idea that I, the lowly constituent, am prone to mistake my own interests (perhaps because I am incapable of thinking about the overall welfare), but it is in the hands of my wise and all-seeing representative to reinterpret my choices because, of course, she knows far better than me what I want or, at least, how to get it.

Plotke is entitled to reply that this is a caricature. Perhaps it is, just as Berlin (as he himself would acknowledge) caricatures the doctrine of positive liberty in various writers to highlight its most extreme and dangerous form and how it can be misused in the wrong hands. Yet, there is a similar worry here. Representative democracy, and the way it has

---

[126] Madison in Hamilton, Madison and Jay 2003, no. 10 p. 44 (my italics).
[127] See, for example, Hamilton in Hamilton, Madison and Jay 2003, no. 35 pp. 159–160. Cf. Hamilton in Elliot 1861, pp. 301–302.
[128] See especially Plotke 1997, pp. 25–27 where he attacks Benjamin Barber's argument for "strong democracy". "Direct democracy", he concludes, "is implausible – not a desirable but difficult goal, nor an attractive horizon that may be out of reach", p. 27. I return to this argument in part two.
[129] Plotke 1997, p. 29 (my italics). I should also point out, in relation to this, that Plotke rejects mandated representation, p. 31. Compare this quotation from Plotke with Berlin 2002b, pp. 180–181, quoted above, p. 37.

The Problem of Positive Liberty

traditionally been defended, does allow for this kind of argumentation.[130] Lasse Thomassen provides another striking illustration. "The trouble with Tormey's post-representational position", Thomassen says, "is that it is 'vain' and therefore potentially dangerous because it overlooks the role of political and intellectual leadership in formulating what we, or the peoples of Chiapas, really are."[131] This is quite striking language, and it would be interesting to know what Berlin would have made of it as it sounds as though it could easily be Fichte, or even Rousseau.[132]

Plotke himself was well aware that justifications for 'representation' (though clearly not representative democracy) could be little more than a specious veil for tyranny,[133] but still, this link between the doctrine at the heart of the Berlinean conception of positive liberty and supposedly benign (or even in, for example, Madison's case, celebrated) defences of representative government has been comprehensively overlooked and ignored.

There does not necessarily have to be a philosophical link between representative government and positive liberty. You could argue, as many do,[134] for example, that representative government is more desirable than participatory government, because it is more convenient and because participatory democracy is impossible in modern nation-states (though this argument is quickly being rendered obsolete), or you could argue for a form of mandated representation,[135] or you could argue for a form of representation that was decided, among all of us, by lot and not by election. Indeed, many of those

---

[130] Cf. Manin 1997, an excellent account of how representative democracy was defended as a superior form of political organisation precisely because it did not pay attention to the wishes of the people, but instead let their superiors (Harrington and Jefferson's "natural aristocracy"), who were supposed to know the people's interests better than the people themselves, decide everything on behalf of all.

[131] Thomassen 2007, p. 124. He is critiquing Tormey 2006.

[132] Compare, for example, interestingly, Berlin 2002b, p. 184 and ff.

[133] "Peron, or Castro, or even Mussolini represents you because he is like you, understands you, is even identical to you as a part of the people", Plotke 1997, p. 28.

[134] See, for example, pp. 90–91 below.

[135] Note that Plotke rejects this. See n. 129 above. For the mandate-independence controversy see Pitkin 1967, pp. 144–167; Pitkin 1989, p. 142.

who defend(ed) representative government do, and did, use these arguments (though rarely the last one, interestingly), but they also used the argument I have been discussing – i.e. that the mass of the people is, in all essentials, too stupid to govern itself and, therefore, that government should be left to the care of the wise and knowledgeable.[136]

Although I say that there is no inherent philosophical link between representative government and positive liberty arguments, representation does, I think, allow for these kinds of arguments because it is an inherently foggy concept. Just who, or what, is being represented (and of course, why)? Is a choice among (being generous for a moment) seven or eight political parties supposed to be representative of human and popular choice and thought? No views of mine are ever communicated to my 'representative' (although they could be, on occasion, if I attended my representative's constituent surgeries) save for a vote, given once every four or five years, for him or her from the paltry list of alternatives. There is a clear gap between representative and representor and this can lead to problems.

Plotke, for example, worries that certain dictators have used representative arguments to justify horrendous tyranny and have manipulated the concept of representation.[137] Yet, he can still say "physical persons and relations of political representation exist at different analytical levels. Even though these levels are intertwined in actual situations they are not the same. Thus it is plausible to say that in a given context, someone is present politically but not physically."[138] I find this notion, frankly, incomprehensible (as well as potentially dangerous), particularly when the ratio of representative to constituents is something like 1: 50,000. How are these 50,000 people actually 'present', or even represented, when the representative comes to vote in Parliament, especially those who did not vote for their parliamentarian in the first place and are unlikely, therefore, to agree with his or her policies or views?[139] How does the representative actually vote? What

---

[136] Edge (Forthcoming A).
[137] See n. 133 above.
[138] Plotke 1997, p. 30.
[139] Of course, modern representatives do typically point out that they will 'represent' all their constituents. Yet, how could (for example) a

portion of the 50,000 people is "present politically" when the representative votes and in what way? To suggest that I am present somewhere (spiritually, economically, politically, whatever) where I am not, in fact, present and have no personal voice at all, is not all that dissimilar to a doctrine of a second, or 'real', self and is open to manipulation in the same way (especially when coupled with the sort of arguments I have been discussing above). What stops my 'representative' from arguing that any given decision is what my (so-called) 'political self' has willed, even though my physical self rails and struggles against it with all my might?[140] Is it that we only need to worry about these problems, and this kind of manipulation, when the deceiver is a dictator, or a tyrant doing unjust things? That of course, was clearly not what Berlin himself was saying and, further, the word 'unjust' is here going to cause problems, significant problems in fact. For, what is to count as 'just', and what is to count as 'unjust', and on whose account? There are already – major – problems here.[141]

Thankfully in most cases this argument of mine *is* a caricature, and modern liberal representative governments do not use these kind of arguments to justify horrendous and unjust acts. But it is not a caricature on all levels because, yet again, that word 'unjust' creates problems all of its own. And herein lies the rub.

Yes modern, liberal, representative governments do not impose the kind of horrific life and conditions on their populations like those which occur under fascism, totalitarianism and the worst forms of repression, which Berlin saw as the consequences of positive liberty doctrines. But this cannot be the end of the story. Many unjust conditions do, in fact, endure within the borders of liberal representative polities – homelessness, appalling treatment of asylum seekers and other migrants, ghettoisation and other conditions and situations brought about by the impact of inequality.[142]

---

conservative parliamentarian, who won the election in my constituency, represent me on a vote for a 70% tax levy on the wealthy when I have voted for a socialist candidate? How could I, in all plausibility, be represented, let alone be present 'politically', in this instance?

[140] See Berlin 2002b, pp. 180–181.
[141] See the conclusion, below.
[142] I will discuss these points, together with the relevant literature (which is vast) in part two.

We need not press the example so far that it becomes a similar justification for tyranny to those Berlin was himself concerned with. Should it not trouble us that our representatives do, in fact, frequently make pronouncements about our 'liberty', our 'free countries', our 'free way of life', 'the free world' and so on? What grounds are there for us to take such statements as true? I have just been attempting to suggest what the consequences of our accepting such pronouncements on trust might be. Why should we believe such claims? What is the evidence for them? What, if anything, do we have to go on?

On What We Are

In Thomassen's striking phrase, the representative is involved in the process of deciding what, in fact, "we are". But it is just this kind of language Berlin tells us to be wary of. Yet Thomassen is surely right in the starkness of what he says. Our representatives are heavily involved in deciding what 'we are', how we should live and the kind of laws, policies, procedures, rights and entitlements (together with a variety of other things) needed to ensure that that way of life is protected and guaranteed.

At no point in historical time have we, the people, been given the choice (in any meaningful sense) on whether or not we agree. On whether, for example, we happen to think that living under nation-state capitalism, protected by government by representation, is the best reflection of who 'we are'. And, of course, this judgement, together with vast numbers of other judgements by our representatives, takes positions on many aspects of the human situation, on human life and human interaction and on human rationality.

It is interesting (if not all that surprising) that one of the few uncontroversial aspects of Berlin's argument in 'Two Concepts of Liberty' has been the concerns he outlined regarding the consequences of (what Berlin called) positive liberty doctrines.[143] It is hard not to agree. The identification of (so-called) human truth, whether that be true freedom, true

---

[143] I do not wish to imply that what Berlin conceived to be positive liberty was not itself highly controversial. A neat survey of the literature is provided by Harris 2002, and the starting point remains, as always, MacCallum 1967.

happiness, justice or peace, with some subjective interpretation of those concepts, based on a subjective and questionable view of what constitutes true human nature, or rationality, is to start down the dark road to tyranny and oppression. As I have been pointing out, liberal, representative, nation-state and capitalist polities of the first decade of the twenty-first century can hardly be compared to Hitler's Germany, Mussolini's Italy or Stalin's Russia (for example), but that does not, in itself, eliminate the consequences Berlin himself identified as emanating from these kinds of arguments. It may also be that we come to look back on these times, and on the consequences of inequality we allow to endure,[144] as flagrantly amoral, if not quite to the same degree as the consequences of totalitarianism.

It seems to me that the only way to avoid the kind of consequences Berlin himself identified is to stop making subjective judgements about human rationality and to let human rationality and judgement speak for itself, at least as far as this is possible.[145] Or, more correctly, we should be allowed to say for ourselves what 'we are', rather than being told what it is in our best interests to want and desire and how best to achieve our wishes and desires, by our representatives and, indeed, our political philosophers.[146] This raises huge problems that I wish, in no way, to ignore or downplay, but, if we are to avoid the pitfalls to human unfreedom Berlin himself identified then, regardless of the difficulty of the task and the problems it may pose, we might not have a choice, no matter how unpalatable the consequences may be for some. I see this as the first part of the 'naturalisation' (to shamefully borrow a phrase from W.V. Quine[147]) of political philosophy. This is the essence of the current project – that the judging of those fundamental questions of political philosophy I began with, will be best done by each of us and not on our behalf, by others.

To put it succinctly, what a great deal of representative

---

[144] See p. 111 below for some examples.
[145] Some of the problems with this are discussed below.
[146] I try to provide some interesting examples of this on pp. 87–93 below.
[147] From Quine 1969a.

theory has denied is, essentially, first-person authority, at least in certain important regards. This is the idea embodied in Wittgenstein's statement "no one can think a thought for me in the way that no one can don my hat for me."[148] This is the essence of first-person authority, as brilliantly explored by Donald Davidson (among others), the principle that no one can know my own mind better than I know it myself. As Davidson succinctly put it, "we know in a way no one else can what we believe, fear, want, value and intend."[149]

This gives rise to the obvious and basic intuition that the best person to judge how I am to live my life is me and me alone. It seems then, an odd step to deny, what a vast amount of the history of political thought has denied,[150] that the mass of the people do not possess the insight or rationality enough to undertake this task. The notion that politics – how I am to be governed and why – is complex, mysterious and beyond the comprehension of most of us simple beings living outside of parliament is not, of course, far removed from those I have just been considering. I might need access to better information, better tools and better evidence than I currently possess to undertake this task to the best of my abilities, and to undertake it freely (indeed, I shall come back to this point), but to suggest that it is a task beyond my means is not only a clear misrepresentation of everyday life, it is also, as I have tried to show, to start down the dark road to tyranny. As Berlin very eloquently puts it

> the doctrine that accumulations of power can never be too great,

---

[148] Wittgenstein 1980, p. 2. Or, as it was put by a radical democratic writer, John Oswald, towards the end of the eighteenth century in a very different context: "I confess that I have never been able to consider this representative system, without wondering at the easy credulity with which the human mind swallows the most palpable absurdities. Were a man seriously to propose, that the nation should piss by proxy, he would doubtless be regarded as a madman. But the fact is, that although we cannot think for each other any more than we can love for each other, or eat and drink for each other, yet, by the habit of delegating to others the task of thinking for us, we insensibly learn to think altogether." Oswald 1995, p. 96.

[149] Davidson 2001b, p. 193. This idea is discussed and explored in pretty much all of the essays in Davidson 2001b, often from the perspective of 'triangulation', discussed below, pp. 62 ff.

[150] See Edge (Forthcoming A).

provided that they are rationally controlled and used, ignores the central reason for pursuing liberty in the first place – that all paternalist governments, however benevolent, cautious, disinterested and rational, have tended, in the end, to treat the majority of men as minors, or as being too often incurably foolish or irresponsible; or else as maturing so slowly as not to justify their liberation at any clearly foreseeable date … This is a policy which degrades men, and seems to me to rest on no rational or scientific foundation, but, on the contrary, on a profoundly mistaken view of the deepest human needs.[151]

It is I think, at this level where the Athenian democratic insight is so valuable. The Athenian theory provides a very rare and interesting argument about the merits of first-person authority in political life. As Thucydides has the (so-called) radical democrat Cleon very bluntly put it, "cities are governed better by the man on the street."[152] Or, as Thucydides' Perikles says, "nor does poverty bar the way [to political involvement], if a man has it in him to be of service to the state, he is not hindered by the obscurity of his condition."[153] Even Plato, ever hostile to democracy, was at least prepared to admit that the Athenians were wise to listen to those who were skilled in the matter that was before the assembly – whether that was shipbuilders for matters relating (if it is not too obvious to say) to harbours and shipbuilding, to generals for military matters and so on.[154]

This natural stress on first-person authority, leading to the recognition of equal ability in the political arena, provides the natural way out of Berlin's problem of positive freedom since it wholeheartedly rejects the idea that human beings are so 'incurably foolish' that they have to be watched over by others and that decisions about who 'we are', and regarding what that means for our ongoing cooperation in society, need to be made by those wiser than ourselves. All are equal in knowing what it is in each of our own best interests to want, desire, intend and need.

---

[151] Berlin 2002a, p. 54.
[152] Thucydides. 3. 37.
[153] Thucydides 2. 37.
[154] Plato *Protagoras* 319 b-d.

First-Person Authority

What the greatest liberal writers, Berlin amongst them, have understood so well is that the recognition of first-person authority is basic to individual freedom. Indeed, this is the essence of liberal negative freedom, the heart of Mill's idea that each and every individual needs a realm, privileged as his or her own, free from interference by others and by the state, where he or she is free to go his or her own way and do his or her own thing.

Perhaps what Berlin and his fellow liberals have not understood so well is all of the many ways in which first-person authority can be undermined, and undermined by both language and its users, human beings, who make all kinds of judgements – in our stead – about how wide that area for free movement should be and why. As I have been saying, this is not only called 'freedom' in the modern world, but it has also, traditionally, been defended by the kinds of argument Berlin himself identified as being at the heart of all positive liberty doctrines which deny first-person authority.

I will now move on to discuss some (but by no means all) of the many ways in which first-person authority can be undermined and why, as a result of that, we should continue to be wary of positive liberty doctrines and their consequences. This is the next stage in the 'naturalisation' of political philosophy – once first-person authority has been acknowledged and, indeed, given some authority, how can it be supported so that the freedom of the mental is expanded and developed? These are important and complex issues, but if I am right, it should be down to all of us to judge those issues and how they relate to what we are.

Chapter Three
Language, Knowledge, Rationality
The Naturalisation of Political Philosophy

Introduction

I have suggested that political philosophy should be 'naturalised'. I have suggested that part of the answer to this lies in first-person authority and its political consequences, meaning that it should be left to each of us to judge the form of socio-political organisation we would most like to live under, according to how those different forms of socio-political organisation are described by principles of justice and/or according to how those different organisations strike a chord with us as rational, as well as moral, beings. However, I have also suggested that there will be a number of problems with this situation which we will need to overcome. In this chapter, I will discuss the second part of naturalisation, which relates to a number of those issues and how we can help to overcome them.

This will focus on the language-picture[155] we have inherited from our ancestors and predecessors. In other words, what we need to focus on is our contemporary normative language-picture and the ways in which it contains the accumulated jumble of views, beliefs, thoughts and values of our ancestors and predecessors and on how we come to learn, and internalise, our political and moral language. The reason for doing so seems to me to be twofold. Firstly, this is the level – language – at which all contributions to the process I am outlining here must, inevitably, be aimed. Secondly, it is hoped that an understanding of our language-picture, and the beliefs and meanings it carries, will hope to free our judgement, both regarding that language-picture itself and regarding the process which I have described above, i.e. our

---

[155] Cf. Wittgenstein 2001, § 115 p. 41, § 139 p. 46. Cf. II xi pp. 171 ff.

choosing the form of political and social organisation we wish to live under.

Rawls said that a conception of justice should start by looking at the shared public conceptions of a democratic society, to help build a conception of justice acceptable to the members of that society as free and equal citizens, yet each with competing conceptions of the good. He says, "we start then, by looking to the public culture itself as the shared fund of implicitly recognised basic ideas and principles".[156] On one level it is hard not to agree,[157] but, as we saw in chapter one, those values, concepts and ideas can be understood in different ways from the hegemonal, or orthodox, account contained in the language-picture, and arguably more significantly, other cultures (and even other times), might have different readings or understandings of those concepts as well.

Unless we encounter these alternative versions of the orthodox linguistic use of the concept, we will not know how far they might reflect what 'we are', or what we believe ourselves to be. Further, the language-picture we have inherited, as we shall see, contains any number of views, thoughts, biases, theories and prejudices (about political and moral matters) which, when we examine them in any detail (as I am suggesting via the structure I am here proposing), we might happen to disagree with. This, indeed, is key. Whilst there is clearly a sense in which that language-picture *will*, to some extent, reflect our deepest needs and interests,[158] how far it actually does so, particularly when it comes to our moral and political concepts, is up for debate. In other words, before we start building those concepts of justice, or the political society described by those concepts, as I hope to have shown in chapter one, we need to start by investigating the language-picture itself and investigating how far it does reflect what we 'are'. Otherwise, the danger is that, not only might we continue to endorse social conditions which are far from just,[159] further, as Berlin's argument regarding positive liberty reminds us, we might come to inhabit social and political conditions and socio-economic relationships which

---
[156] Rawls 1996, § 1.3 p. 8. See also (for example) Rawls 1996, p. 306.
[157] See pp. 61–69 below.
[158] See pp. 104–107 below.
[159] Cf. Rawls 2001, n. 4 p. 4.

Language, Knowledge, Rationality

define those conditions. These are (or may be), in fact, based upon collective prejudices, thoughts, views and theories on what it is rational for us as human beings to want, to do and, as we have seen, to 'be'. Yet the thinkers who suggested these beliefs on what it is rational for human beings to want, and on the form of social organisation under which we, as rational beings, will fare best may simply have been wrong regarding vital matters relating to the political. It is worth our remembering Berlin's words from the previous chapter.[160] Have we been treated as so 'incurably foolish', and what in turn might this mean for our individual freedom?

In other words, this is political philosophy attempting to fulfil a role which Wittgenstein posited for philosophy in general. Philosophy he said, "is a battle against the bewitchment of our intelligence by means of our language."[161] Quentin Skinner has said much the same thing and interestingly, in similar terminology.

> It is remarkably difficult, [Skinner writes], to avoid falling under the spell of our own intellectual heritage. As we analyse and reflect on our own normative concepts, it is easy to become bewitched into believing that the ways of thinking about them bequeathed to us by the mainstream of our intellectual traditions, must be *the* ways of thinking about them ... The intellectual historian can help us to appreciate how far the values embodied in our present way of life, and our present ways of thinking about those values, reflect a series of choices made at different times between different possible worlds. This awareness can help to liberate us from the grip of any one hegemonal account of those values and how they should be interpreted and understood.[162]

I could not agree more.

As I have shown in chapter one, a given normative concept (in this case freedom) tends to be accompanied by any number of beliefs, thoughts, theories and prejudices (as well as related things). Some may be more controversial than others, but none represent the (naked) concept itself, though they are certainly

---

[160] See pp. 48–49 above.
[161] Wittgenstein 2001, § 109 p. 40.
[162] Skinner 1998, pp. 116–117.

related. As Skinner says, an investigation into this language-picture is likely to free our judgement, since we will see the kind of linguistic battles and scraps that have been fought over our normative concepts (and there are many) and, over those 'different possible worlds'. This is an especially useful task when, as I am suggesting here, we need to start thinking again about those different possible worlds and what we might want from them and/or what we might even be owed from them. By seeing these concepts, values, beliefs and thoughts for what they are – as subjective interventions into an unending dispute over the ways human beings should (in both senses) live their lives and over the conditions under which they can best do so – it can be hoped that we might be freer to judge whether they are, after all, accurate reflections of what 'we are' and subsequently, freer to judge how, if at all, we would like to amend things. Which of those 'different possible worlds' might appeal to us as rational and/or moral beings, trying to decide how we might best live our lives, engaged in social cooperation over time with our fellow human beings?

Mind, Word and World

What in other words troubles me, are statements like the following:

> Of course language reflects our native interests and our historically accumulated needs and values, our built-in and learned dispositions. But this fact hardly supports the claim that language seriously distorts or shapes our understanding of the world; the influence, such as it is, goes the other way. The most we are entitled to say is that as individuals we happily inhabit culturally evolved categories we personally did little to devise. In this case, language does not distort; rather, society gives us a leg up on coping with the environment it partly constitutes.[163]

Giving an example, Davidson goes on, "my language may (or

---
[163] Davidson 2005, p. 129. There is clearly an aspect about this about which Davidson is – fundamentally – right (see pp. 61–69 below), but language (and/or its users) does distort and it does so in a number of complex and dynamic ways. How much it distorts (and where the distortion occurs) is, of course, seriously open to debate, though I am not generally concerned with this here, but see n. 165 below.

may not) have something to do with my, or society's interest in the question whether the clearing of tropical forests is speeding the destruction of the ozone layer, but language has nothing to do with the truth of the matter."[164] But language has everything to do with the truth of the matter, since only it (and no other vehicle) carries the truth-value of a sentence.[165]

In fact, the thought (like, for example) 'the destruction of the rainforests speeds up the thinning of the ozone layer', would not even exist were it not for language, since among other things, it is clear, as Davidson well knows, that the ability to think it depends on our having a vast number of other beliefs.[166] Without language, there is no concept of truth, nor, as Davidson would argue (and I would agree), thought.[167] As he explains elsewhere

> I have wanted to concentrate on what seems to me primary and so apt to go unnoticed: the necessary degree of commonality essential to understanding another individual, and the extent to which such understanding provides the foundation of the concept of truth and reality upon which all thought depends ...[168]

Or to put the matter more simply, truth is, fundamentally, an intersubjective standard.[169] Meanings, as Hilary Putnam famously put it in a well worn phrase, ain't in the head.

This is an essential point to grasp. "Language," to quote

---

[164] Davidson 2005, p. 129. I find this statement very surprising given Davidson's own – utterly brilliant – account of the intersubjective nature of knowledge. See below.

[165] E.g., Quine 1980b, p. 36: "It is obvious that truth in general depends on both language and extralinguistic fact. The statement 'Brutus killed Caesar' would be false if the world had been different in certain ways, but it would also be false if the word 'killed' happened rather to have the sense of 'begat'." I am not here interested in whether the distortion is in the sentence, the proposition, the judgement, or something else, only in the fact that all of these, following the speaker's pronouncement of belief, are carried by language, and nothing else. In other words, whether you want to hold that the distortion is caused by meaning, by judgement, by proposition, by speaker or by sentence, language, ultimately, carries that distortion from one speaker to the next in the causal way described. Or, of course, it doesn't.

[166] See, for example, Davidson 2004, pp. 9 ff.

[167] See Davidson 2001b essays 7 and 9, for example.

[168] Davidson 2001b, p. 219.

[169] E.g. Davidson 2001b, p. 191.

Davidson again, "is in its nature, as Neurath insisted, intersubjective; what someone else's words mean on a given occasion is always something that we can in principle learn from public clues."[170] In other words, language has, to return to Davidson's example, a great deal to do with the truth of the statement 'the destruction of the rainforests speeds up the thinning of the ozone layer', since it is through language (through conversation with others) that we learn the correct application of the terms 'destruction', 'rainforests' and 'ozone layer', as well as the vast array of other beliefs we must necessarily hold in order for us to successfully interpret that statement if and when we hear it.

Now, let us say that a scientist carries out a study on whether the clearing of the rainforests is actually speeding up the thinning of the ozone layer. What happens? She studies the matter, conducts experiments, collects data and writes a report which is then circulated within the government (which has, for sake of argument, commissioned it). Let us say that she ignores (or overlooks, or misinterprets) the findings of the evidence and concludes that there is in fact, no such connection between the two phenomena and subsequently, this is what the government, through various media, circulates to the general public. The general public then come to accept the statement 'the clearing of the rainforests has nothing to do with the thinning of the ozone layer' as true.

A further problem is that a great deal can – and should – be said about this. Firstly, what are the intentions of the scientist? What if she has been paid by the government (at the behest of the property development lobby) and told to look at her data in a certain way (or perhaps she has been selected because of the way she looks at certain data)? What if she has been deliberately mischievous in her writing of the report? What if she is just not a very good scientist? It might, then, justifiably be objected that it is not language, as such, that is at fault, but its users. As true as this is, it still does not affect the conclusion that language is providing us (say the public in this case) with a (seriously) distorted picture of the world. Further, in this case it is (potentially) a dramatic distortion, one with (potentially) devastating consequences for the human race, if,

---

[170] Davidson 2001b, p. 174.

that is, the scientist's claim is actually false.

Of course, the real, empirical, situation in this regard is very different. It cannot come down to one scientist writing a report, thereby causing the rest of us to take everything she says as true. Equally, of course, this example puts a notably unreal slur on the reputations of most scientists, who do not generally carry on in the way our scientist does. What tends to happen is something akin to a battle. Scientists, coming from various different perspectives with different data, and attached to various different organisations, are engaged in the process of attempting to win over our minds to their particular views on the matter. In other words, this is not wholly unlike the ongoing battle over our ethical and normative concepts where others attempt, very simply and in a basic sense, to persuade us to see the world their way.[171] Though of course good science (like good political and moral philosophy in fact) will ultimately leave little room for dispute.

A problem comes when I ask 'who am I to believe and why?'[172] Indeed, what do I have to go on? What grounds are there for my believing this statement, or that one, to be true? As Wittgenstein put it, "we just *can't* investigate everything, and for that reason we are forced to rest content with assumption. If I want the door to turn, the hinges must stay put."[173] I am no scientist and, therefore, am forced to accept that scientists, generally speaking, are not lying to me.[174] I personally have no means of investigating or questioning the evidence they provide as the basis for their views, even if I can understand a number of the basic essentials in relation to that evidence.[175] Putnam put this very neatly when he said, "there is, in connection with many terms, a *linguistic division of labour*. What I refer to as an 'elm' is, with my consent, and that of my linguistic community, what people who can distinguish elms from other trees refer to as an elm."[176]

---

[171] See the insightful comments of Skinner in Skinner 2002, pp. 6–7.
[172] Cf. Quine 1980b, pp. 44–45.
[173] Wittgenstein 1974, 343 p. 44. Cf. 344 p. 44: "My *life* consists in my being content to accept many things."
[174] See, importantly, Quine 1980b, p. 44.
[175] Cf., the quotation from Quine, p. 66 below.
[176] Putnam 1975b, p. 274. Although, I would add that there is a very interesting use of the word "consent" here.

This is also very much the situation regarding our political and moral beliefs, principles and values and with that, regarding the different forms of socio-political organism, Skinner's 'different possible worlds', described by these.[177] What I refer to as 'liberty', what I refer to as 'democracy', 'justice', 'rights', and so on, is what those members of my linguistic community who are involved in providing analyses of such things have settled on. Or, as it may well be, we *use* those applications of concepts that have been victorious on the bloody battlefield of linguistic conflict.[178] At least, this is the case generally speaking. And so in chapter one, we saw the liberal interpretation of liberty which has become victorious.[179] In other words, liberal writers have been very successful in convincing us that their analysis of liberty, complete with all the accompanying beliefs and positions they take in relation to it, is the best way of using the word. Though, of course, 'convincing us' is a curious and controversial phrase, as the actual process by which any given interpretation, or use, of a concept becomes victorious, or hegemonic, is, at the deeper level anyway, notably mysterious.[180] It is (partly) this which the present project is attempting to redress.

The fact that the liberal conception of freedom (for example) *has* become victorious, has a number of significant corollaries. For one, it means that this will be the usage of the word 'freedom' we will tend to come across, and so it proves.[181] We should bear in mind here Davidson's argument that we need to free ourselves from the notion that thought-processes must be mysterious.

Davidson writes

When we have freed ourselves from the assumption that thoughts must have mysterious objects, we can see how the fact that mental states as we commonly conceive them are identified

---

[177] N.B., for example, Skinner's comments on the history of our political and ethical ideas more than resembling a battlefield (with I might add, many unfortunate casualties). See Skinner 2002a, p. 7.
[178] See below.
[179] See Skinner 1998, pp. 97 ff. See also Edge 2009 and (Forthcoming B).
[180] See for example, the interesting example provided by Skinner in Skinner 1998, pp. 97 ff. Cf. Edge 2009, pp. 36–37, for another such example. Though both of these examples do not go beyond the superficial, as it were.
[181] Cf., for example, Brown 2007.

in part by their natural history not only fails to touch the internal character of such states or to threaten first person authority; it also opens the way to an explanation of first person authority. The explanation comes with the realisation that what a person's words mean depends in the most basic cases on the kinds of objects and events that have caused the person to hold the words to be applicable; similarly for what the person's thoughts are about.[182]

What we must get away from (though we might already be far away from it, I have no wish to argue against straw people) is the notion of 'false consciousness'. To the contrary, we often have good reasons for believing what we believe and this, as I am seeing it, is the whole problem. It is not, in other words, that a false 'scheme' is hiding the true 'reality' from our view.[183]

For now, simply consider whether I am any better off regarding the debate over how many species of Elm there are (owing to the complexities of hybridisation), than I am regarding the complex debates about freedom, democracy and justice (for example). Unless, of course, there is some kind of causal bridge between mind, word and world involved. In other words, I will have to learn about freedom, coercion and restraint, just as I will have learned about Elms and hybridisation. Further, on the deeper level, I will have had to encounter the disputes over these concepts and things and what those disputes are about if I am to begin questioning those concepts and how they relate to my world, and to my place in the moral and political universe which surrounds me. Though, generally speaking, unless I am interested in these matters, either as a 'layperson' or, even more rarely, as a professional or academic, I will, fundamentally, be reliant on Putnam's division of linguistic labour and the complex linguistic processes and battles I have described which lie behind it. I have to rely on botanists on the classification of Elms, regarding the problems of hybridisation, just as I have to rely on politicians and political theorists[184] for 'liberty',

---

[182] Davidson 2001b, p.37.
[183] Or, the 'third dogma of empiricism', attacked in Davidson 2001a, pp. 183–198. Cf., Quine's reply in Quine 1981a. I return to these issues shortly.
[184] Though, to what degree on each? This is an interesting problem. Note

regarding problems like coercion, restraint, human ability and the division of labour in relation to equality and resources. In other words, it is influential texts, such as Berlin's, which will come to have an important impact on these matters.

Viewing a thought as nothing more complex than this kind of causal bridge has one further aspect which needs to be considered. It is that "thoughts require a history. Not only must an object capable of thought be capable of learning: it must have learned a great deal. A creature or object cannot have a thought about stars or squid or sawdust unless that thought somehow traces back causally to appropriate examples."[185] Quine gives a simple example of what I am driving at. "Consider, to begin with, the observation sentence 'It's raining'. Tom is learning it from Martha by ostension. Martha's business is to encourage Tom in uttering the sentence, or in assenting to it, when she sees that he is noticing appropriate phenomena, and to discourage him otherwise."[186]

One of the problems is that this situation inevitably becomes more complex when it comes to our normative vocabularies. As Wittgenstein explained at the beginning of the *Philosophical Investigations*, "if you describe the learning of a language in this way [ostension] you are, I believe, thinking primarily of nouns like "table", "chair", "loaf", and of people's names, and only secondarily of the names of certain actions and properties; and of the remaining kinds of words as something that will take care of itself."[187] We simply don't know enough about how, and when, we acquire our normative vocabularies (assuming that we do acquire them, at least in the basic semantic sense). It is certainly not easy to imagine Martha and Tom sitting down to learn, ostensively, 'liberty', 'democracy' and 'justice', at least certainly not until

---

Skinner's recent point on his own project, that "this attempt to rewrite the history of negative liberty has not so far had any influence that I know of on public life." Skinner 2005a, p. 3.

[185] Davidson 2004, p. 88.
[186] Quine 1992, §24 p. 61. Or, Davidson 2001b, p. 174 (for example): "Consider how we discover what some simple sentence means, say 'There's a table' or 'Here's a piece of green paper'. Our basic evidence is that the speaker is caused to assent (not just on this occasion, but generally) to these sentences by the presence of tables or pieces of green paper, while the absence of these objects causes him (generally) to dissent from the same sentences." Cf. Davidson 2001b, p. 189.
[187] Wittgenstein 2001, § 1, p. 2.

later in Tom's life. Yet, somehow, somewhere, a causal bridge must be involved for those of us, the great majority of us, who do acquire this kind of vocabulary. Though at what stage and with what depth, do we make contact with our normative concepts?

Regarding the matter at hand, a further problem arises. This is again hinted at by Quine during Martha and Tom's exchange. "Observation sentences," Quine goes on, "learned ostensively, are where our command of language begins, and our learning them depends heavily on the ability of our elders to guess that we are getting the appropriate perception."[188] And it is our elders' own "appropriate perception" which is significant here, as this will depend on what they themselves understand by the meanings of the words involved. Very basically then, what we come to learn as 'democracy', as 'liberty', as 'justice' and so on, will in great part depend, in everyday discourse at least, on what our society understands by these terms, and on what it has accepted as their meaning (use), since this will be how our elders will understand and employ these concepts. Again, I hope that chapter one has provided a significant example of what this means in practice.

Our contemporary language-picture just does not reflect this kind of controversy and this kind of conflict and it never will, unless we want to start speaking in a hopelessly unwieldy, pseudo-scientific way, which it is doubtful that we ever would, or indeed should.[189] Therefore, we are, and always will be, left vulnerable to the complexities, eccentricities, confusions and distortions of language. It is worth emphasising again that this is not about 'false consciousness', or the hope that the 'true' conceptual scheme is waiting just over the horizon, to be discovered by historical and philosophical enquiry. Far from it. The problem is much more sophisticated, much more complex and much more subtle.

Intersubjectivity

Readers might think that I have given myself a problem. For, on the one hand, I have rejected out of hand the notion of 'false consciousness' yet, on the other, I am claiming that we

---
[188] Quine 1992, §24 p. 61.
[189] Cf. Davidson 2001a, p. 188.

should be wary of our inherited language-picture, because it may well be carrying a multiplicity of judgements and standpoints which, when we come to it, we might reject during the kind of process I am outlining here. Let me say something more about these complexities.

I am in full agreement with Davidson that the vast majority of our beliefs cannot be wrong.[190] What Davidson's account of the intersubjective nature of knowledge explains so brilliantly (and so radically) is that we share a world with one another, the larger features of which must, generally speaking, be true. This is the essence of Davidson's theory of triangulation.

Davidson explains

> I have wanted to concentrate on what seems to me to be primary and so apt to go unnoticed: the necessary degree of commonality essential to understanding another individual and the extent to which such understanding provides the foundation of the concept of truth and reality upon which all thought depends … what is certain is that the clarity and effectiveness of our concepts grows with the growth of our understanding of others … If I am right, our propositional knowledge has its basis not in the impersonal but in the interpersonal. Thus, when we look at the natural world we share with others, we do not lose contact with ourselves, but rather acknowledge membership in a society of minds. If I did not know what others think, I would have no thoughts of my own and so would not know what I think. If I did not know what I think, I would lack the ability to gauge the thoughts of others. Gauging the thoughts of others requires that I live in the same world as them, sharing many reactions to its major features, including its values. So there is no danger that in viewing the world objectively we will lose touch with ourselves. The three sorts of knowledge form a tripod: if any leg were lost, no part would stand.[191]

This argument, as Richard Rorty pointed out, has radical

---

[190] See, for example, Davidson 2001a, pp. 183–198, esp. pp. 196–198. See also the essays in Davidson 2001b with above.

[191] Davidson 2001b, pp. 219–220. The anti-Cartesian nature of this theory is brought out very clearly, together with its radical implications for (all branches of) contemporary philosophy, by Davidson 2004, pp. 3–18. See also the warm review by Rorty (Rorty 2005), which I (briefly) discussed in the preface above.

implications.[192] This partly relates not just to our moral and political values, but to the 'society of minds' who, as Davidson points out, must share those values, in their larger features at least.[193] The implications of this are not Kantian, as Bill Martin, analysing Davidson's ethical thought believed,[194] but arguably much more radical.

Many philosophers have doubted the objective nature of our values and our value judgements. In two famous examples, J.L. Mackie denied that they were part of the 'fabric of the world'[195] and A.J. Ayer thought they were little else than metaphysical hogwash.[196] The subtitle of Mackie's part is, famously, *Inventing Right and Wrong*.

However, David Hume had already provided a rather compelling answer to the doubts Mackie identified some two hundred years previous

> From the apparent usefulness of the social virtues", Hume pointed out, "it has readily been inferred by sceptics, both ancient and modern, that all moral distinctions arise from education, and were, at first, invented, and afterwards encouraged, by the art of politicians in order to render men tractable, and subdue their natural ferocity and selfishness, which incapacitated them for society. This principle, indeed, of precept and education, must so far be owned to have a powerful influence, that it may frequently increase or diminish, beyond their natural standards, the sentiments of approbation or dislike; and may even, in particular cases, create, without any natural principle, a new sentiment of this kind; as is evident in all superstitious practices and observances: But that *all* moral affection or dislike arises from this origin, will surely never be allowed by an judicious enquirer. Had nature made no such distinction, founded on the original constitution of the mind, the words, *honourable* and *shameful, lovely* and *odious, noble* and *despicable,* had never had place in any language; nor could politicians, had they invented these terms, ever have been able to render them intelligible, or make them convey any idea to the audience."[197]

---

[192] Rorty 2005. Cf. n. 191 above.
[193] See Davidson's own (brilliant) account in Davidson 2004, pp. 39–57.
[194] See Martin 1999 with Davidson's own response, appended to that essay.
[195] Mackie 1977, p. 15 and see ff.
[196] Ayer 2001, pp. 104–126.
[197] Hume 1998, 5.3 p. 105.

Or, as Davidson, a "judicious enquirer" if ever there was one, put it a little more simply

> to understand the speech of another, I must be able to think of the same things she does; I must have her world. I don't have to agree with her in all matters, but in order to disagree we must entertain the same propositions, with the same subject matter and the same concept of truth.[198]

Ayer's account is particularly problematic. Whilst announcing in his introduction that "we may begin by criticising the metaphysical thesis that philosophy affords us knowledge of a reality transcending the world of common sense",[199] he never quite manages to explain away the fact that our values are a (very important) part of common sense, as Hume pointed out. Ayer claimed that our values are not verifiable by some 'empirical test' because they are not open to observation,[200] but that is clearly false.

Imagine that two people observe another person kicking a dog on a road. The same triangle of speaker, interpreter and outside world is involved. They are both likely to agree that this act is 'cruel', just as they are that a 'kick' and a 'dog' are involved.

Davidson concludes

> What makes our judgements of the 'descriptive' properties of things true or false is the fact that the same properties tend to cause the same beliefs in different observers, and when observers differ, we assume there is an explanation ... the same holds for moral values ... Basic to our understanding of the utterances of another speaker is observation of the circumstances in which the speaker, sincerely as far as we can tell, applies a predicate.[201]

Of course, it would be fruitless to say that this doesn't, from time to time, go wrong. Ethical disagreements, even in simple cases like this, are not merely possible, but are a fundamental

---

[198] Davidson 2001b, p. 105.
[199] Ayer 2001, p. 13.
[200] E.g. Ayer 2001, pp. 108–109.
[201] Davidson 2004, pp. 47–48 and see ff. See also my discussion below, pp. 104–107.

part of common sense and everyday language.[202] Merely because it is plausible to maintain that value judgements are objective, this does not logically entail that I (or anyone else) knows how to solve moral disagreements – if only I did. As Davidson himself said, "I wish I were able to declare that I know of a way to decide, in those cases where a decision is called for, what the right decision is, what we ought to do ... But perhaps it will be agreed that the thesis of the objectivity of values is not only worth discussing, but that discussing it may be one way of bringing about agreement on what is now disputed."[203] I shall have more to say about this in a moment.

Part of the problem, is that we don't have the same physical contact with our normative concepts as we do with (say) 'leaf', 'chair', 'table' and 'mama'. We don't, in other words, see 'freedom', 'justice' and 'cruelty' scuttling through the undergrowth like we might do 'rabbit' or 'bird'. However, we might also say that the Battle of Trafalgar, or the death of Caesar, are not a part of the 'fabric' of the world as such, but the evidence for their existence is 'out there' and (for our purposes) 'out there' in interesting ways. And here, of course, what we mean by 'evidence' is an interesting and deep question and one which has vexed historians for eons.

This may all seem off the point since it is not the purpose of this part to prove the objectivity of values, nor can I claim that the preceding (fleeting) argument has achieved that.[204]

---

[202] Cf. Davidson 2004, p. 40.
[203] Davidson 2004, p. 52.
[204] A further counter to Ayer's (and other moral subjectivists') argument concerns the actual structure of ethical language. As Davidson explained, "those who deny that moral judgements have truth values seldom make a serious attempt to explain the semantics of such sentences" (Davidson 2004, p. 48). I don't think that Ayer's own attempt is adequate (though it is not really an attempt to *explain* such semantics). Ayer says that the sentence 'Stealing money is wrong' is equivalent to 'Stealing money!!' (Ayer 2001, p. 110), which it clearly isn't. I doubt that Ayer is even right that, in the second case, "there is nothing said here which can be true or false" (Ayer 2001, p. 110) – there is at least one example to the contrary – but, regardless, the two are not synonymous. Not only are the two words 'is wrong' missing in the second case, meaning that the statement could be interpreted in at least two different ways, Ayer explains neither why, in common sense (see above), the words 'is wrong' are not replaced by the double exclamation mark nor, more importantly, why 'is wrong' is, in the first place, generally used in ordinary ethical language of this kind. Indeed, the fact that 'right'

There are a number of reasons why I mention it. Not only is it a highly significant part of Davidson's theory, it is also relevant to the current project in a number of ways. Many of these relate to that elusive phrase of Mackie's, regarding what we can find in the 'fabric of the world'.

Davidson himself thought that this was (a response to) a bad question.[205] The reason is because, as Quine radically concluded in his seminal article, 'Two Dogmas of Empiricism', "the totality of our so-called knowledge or beliefs, from the most causal matters of geography and history to the profoundest laws of atomic physics or even of pure mathematics and logic, is a man-made fabric which impinges on experience only along the edges."[206] As Skinner neatly put it, "there is no such 'unvarnished news' to report."[207]

In other words, our moral values come to us, just like anything else, via human interpretation and the notion of an uninterpreted given is one we should give up.[208] To quote an incendiary passage from Quine

> as an empiricist I continue to think of the conceptual scheme of science as a tool, ultimately, for predicting future experience in the light of past experience. Physical objects are conceptually imported into the situation as convenient intermediaries – not by definition in terms of experience, but simply as irreducible posits comparable, epistemologically, to the gods of Homer. For my part I do, qua lay physicist, believe in physical objects and not in Homer's gods; and I consider it a scientific error to believe otherwise. But in point of epistemological footing the physical objects and the gods differ only in degree and not in kind. Both sorts of entities enter our conception only as cultural posits.[209]

However, Davidson's account of triangulation has shown that this situation does not, and need not, impinge upon objectivity – "the source of the concept of objective truth is interpersonal

---

and 'wrong' are used in ethical propositions in much the same way (in the basic semantic sense) as they are in mathematical propositions (for example), needs serious explanation, as Davidson points out.

[205] Davidson 2004, p. 45 – see also the remarks at the top of p. 44.
[206] Quine 1980b, p. 42. See also Putnam 2002, pp. 1–45.
[207] Skinner 2002a, p. 2.
[208] Cf. (for example) Davidson 2001b, pp. 174–175.
[209] Quine 1980b, p. 44.

Language, Knowledge, Rationality 67

communication. Thought depends on communication."[210] Not only does this provide the basis for disagreement in the first place,[211] it also helps us to see how error comes to be identified and as a result our language-picture modified, though error is certainly possible.

As Quine explained, "total science is like a field of force whose boundary conditions are experience. A conflict with experience at the periphery occasions readjustments in the interior of the field. Truth values have to be redistributed over some of our statements."[212] The same is true of our moral and political values – they too are 'refined' by new discoveries and experiments. We come to adjust our language-picture and its truth-values in relation to our political and moral values just as we do with scientific and mathematical truth.

What all this implies, is that we will inherit a language-picture which will be right or wrong in various ways and which will greatly affect what it is rational for us to believe at the given moment we stand, as thinking and judging human beings in the world. So for example, Skinner acknowledges that it is interesting that so eminent a thinker as Jean Bodin believed that there were witches who were in league with the devil.[213]

> Living in the twenty-first century, we are likely to feel ... that these claims are simply false ... If we begin by focusing on such beliefs, we shall provide ourselves with a good starting-point for investigating the structure of ... Bodin's thought ... Whatever account we provide will have to include an explanation of the fact that such admittedly bizarre beliefs nevertheless commended themselves to such unquestionably distinguished minds.[214]

The reason is that, given the language-picture Bodin himself inherited, it was rational for him to believe in witches.[215]

To return to the present example, I cannot say which of our beliefs may turn out to be false because I, together with my

---
[210] Davidson 2001b, p. 209.
[211] E.g. Davidson 2001a, pp. 196–197.
[212] Quine 1980b, p. 42 and see ff.
[213] Skinner 2002a, p. 28.
[214] Skinner 2002a, p. 28.
[215] Skinner 2002a, p. 51.

fellow human beings, have a grasp of the concept of objective truth, which means that I understand that the right (or wrong) answers are logically independent of what I happen to believe. That said, all this does in fact, provide a clear and strong motive for us to investigate our inherited language-picture in the manner I am describing and for obvious reasons. Given that the accumulated collection of thoughts and beliefs contained within our language-picture has a significant impact on what it is, in turn, rational for us to hold, to think and believe, we might want to start questioning all those accumulated assumptions, thoughts and beliefs with greater urgency than we currently do.

This is key. It is wrong, if not dangerous, to simply dismiss individuals as irrational, the blind, ignorant victims of false consciousness, or the false conceptual scheme and, as Berlin so passionately argued, to paint yourself as the liberator.[216] We may often have very good reasons for believing what we believe. For example, despite the arguments to the contrary I mentioned in chapter one, we still have good reasons for believing ourselves to be 'free'. For instance, if we live in one of the so-called 'prosperous democracies', we possess a bundle of individual rights, live (generally) under conditions of free speech and toleration and are not (generally) subject to arbitrary arrest.[217] If we take 'democracy', we (for example) elect our representatives, if infrequently, and are subject (in theory) only to the laws they make and not to the power of a king or queen or an aristocracy. Even in arguably more complex cases, like 'justice' and 'equality', there is similar evidence to suggest that these concepts have some basis in reality, though again, what constitutes evidence here is an interesting question.

One vital corollary of this is that, if we believe the contemporary *use* of our normative concepts to be wrong in certain ways, we must persuade others, through open argument and discussion, that we are right and that, in turn, the alternative form of political organisation we ascribe to – as described by our interpretation of those normative concepts – is the one you (and everyone else) should accept,

---
[216] See chapter two above.
[217] But cf. the warnings provided by Skinner 2003, p. 25.

either as the rational choice, or the moral choice, or (as I will argue) both. This means, as I have said, not only investigating the contemporary language-picture and how it uses those concepts (and all the values, positions, theories and judgements which underlie that use[218]) but also outlining (as far as possible) how the alternative vision(s) will look. Perhaps Engels was right to lament that Marx never left a concrete vision of how he thought post-revolutionary communism would look, though I will have more to say about this in part two. It will have to be rational for human beings to accept an alternative choice, unless the argument over morality can be convincingly won and that is not beyond the realms of possibility. If you can convince others, in large numbers, that a different (in my case more egalitarian) alternative is to be preferred over the present alternative, the revolutionary implications are clear. The same may well go for morality and we can only hope it will.

Thought, Language, Neutrality and Rationality

I must thank readers for being patient, as this has not been easy to get through, but let me now try to bring it all together. Gottlob Frege neatly sums up the basis of what I am trying to get at. In his *Logical Investigations*, Frege asked 'how could a thought act?' His answer was simple yet illuminating

> ... by being grasped and taken to be true ... The influence of man on man is brought about for the most part by thoughts. People communicate thoughts. How do they do this? They bring about changes in the common external world, and these are meant to be perceived by someone else and so give him the chance to grasp a thought and take it to be true. Could the great events of world history have come about without the communication of thoughts?[219]

We stand at the end (or, more properly, our end) of a huge amount of battles, fought both physically and linguistically, over the construction of our shared world and its various

---
[218] I try to provide some further examples of what I mean (aside from those considered in chapter one) below, pp. 89–93.
[219] Frege 1977, pp. 28–29.

components, among them (and primary for my purpose), the political, the social and the economic.

This world we inhabit does not reflect the neutral passage of historical time any more than the doctrines of those thinkers Berlin chastised for believing that they had uncovered the final results of all historical destiny. The world we inhabit reflects an almost incomprehensible jumble of historically accumulated choices, beliefs and prejudices expressed through language. Human beings, as Frege so succinctly pointed out, attempt to persuade others of the truth of what they believe and to (speak) act accordingly. As I have been pointing out, this can have, and is designed to have, a profound effect on our normative concepts.[220]

Another excellent (and very explicit) example of this kind of linguistic battle is provided by F.D. Harvey's superb analysis of the attempts of classical oligarchs to redefine the concept of equality to suit their own purposes.[221] As Harvey says in relation to Aristotle,

> the importance of this passage [Aristotle, *Politics* 1301a26–b4] is that it tells us that equality was the watchword of democrats, and inequality of oligarchs. Not, of course, that oligarchs would have said openly 'Inequality is a splendid thing' – the whole theory of geometric proportion is a subtle attempt to avoid doing just that, an attempt to call inequality "true equality" – but rather that their practice presupposes such an attitude.[222]

When the historical process is openly portrayed like this, as a vast collection of linguistic battles with winners and losers, it can help us to see it for what it really is, and can help to prevent us from, in Skinner's words, being too readily bewitched by the immaculate present that stands in front of us and purports to be some neutral expression of 'the truth'. It is anything but.

Let me give a more contemporary, and arguably more relevant example. Liberalism famously claims to be completely neutral on the question of what the 'good life' for individuals

---

[220] See chapter one above and Edge 2009 and (Forthcoming B). As I have said, this kind of analysis is heavily indebted to that of Skinner.
[221] Harvey 1965.
[222] Harvey 1965, p. 118.

should be. It claims, in other words, that by giving 'equal individual liberty' to those who live under its laws, it allows each of them to pursue their own path and go their own way, without any direction or dictation on the part of the state. This is supposed to allow me to live my life, doing my own good in my own way as I see fit.

A classic and comprehensive recent statement of this idea is Rawls' *Political Liberalism*. Or, as Michael Walzer (briefly) puts it

> the standard liberal argument for neutrality is an induction from social fragmentation. Since dissociated individuals will never agree on the good life, the state must allow them to live as they think best, subject only to John Stuart Mill's harm principle, without endorsing or sponsoring any particular understanding of what 'best' means.[223]

Similar claims are widely visible elsewhere.[224] Berlin's analysis of liberty is an expression of this same idea. Negative liberty is concerned with giving human beings as wide an area as possible for the pursuit of their chosen ends ('How far am I governed?'), whereas freedom's possible totalitarian invader, the positive concept, claims liberty is to be found in a single conception of what a given authority conceives to be the 'good' or 'true' or 'best'.

I am not sure that liberalism is always on the neutral territory here to which it aspires. Liberal democracy, no less than the now redundant forms of what is claimed – misleadingly – to be socialist republics, was the creation of human beings who hold, and held, certain beliefs about human beings (and their interactions with one another) and about the nature of political society and how it should be most effectively (and most rationally) organised, and they attempt(ed) to convince others of their truth.[225] Liberalism,

---

[223] Walzer 1990, p. 16.
[224] See, for example, Dworkin 1978, pp. 122, 128, 142–143. Cf. Rorty 1991, p. 191.
[225] Richard Rorty does, importantly, point out that "both Jefferson and [John] Dewey described America as an 'experiment'. If the experiment fails, our descendants may have learnt something important. But they will not learn a philosophical truth any more than they will learn a religious one. They will simply get some hints about what to watch out for when setting

may make no claim on regulating the 'good life', the free choices of the citizens of liberal democracy, except for the important proviso that this life is led within the confines of liberal society and liberal institutions and all their accompanying laws and structures, as well as beliefs and values on a number of related theories and issues, including, for example, concepts and theories of human rationality, the state, human interaction, morality and of coercion, for example.[226] It is this which is often referred to as "liberty". Liberalism, no more or less than any other ideology or theory, takes positions on what 'we are' and what it is rational for us to do, to want and to accept.

One basic point, itself noted by Rawls, is that "the liberal doctrine was formulated in its main essentials by Constant, Tocqueville and Mill for the context of the modern democratic state which they saw to be imminent."[227] In other words, it *is* a doctrine, an ideology,[228] which, as with all other doctrines, was formulated by individual human beings with very specific motives in mind and with very particular beliefs, fears, prejudices and thoughts accompanying those motives. It did not come out of thin air, as the neutral production of the forces of historical destiny, as Rawls himself acknowledges, but is the product of the kind of very non-neutral linguistic (and physical) battles I have just been describing. Liberals themselves had – and have, as the Berlin example shows[229] –

---

up their next experiment. Even if nothing else survives from the age of democratic revolutions, perhaps our descendants will remember that social institutions *can* be viewed as experiments in cooperation rather than as attempts to embody a universal and ahistorical order", Rorty 1991, p. 196. Naturally I believe that it is very helpful to look at society in this way, but my point is that liberal democracy does not appear to live up to Rorty's claim in practice, even if this is the theory behind it. For one thing, if we are living under, or through, an experiment, where are the opportunities for ending the experiment and experimenting anew?

[226] See above.
[227] Rawls 1996, p. 303.
[228] I do not use this term in a pejorative sense. Liberalism, no more or less than any other theory about what is best for human beings, is a collection of beliefs, theories, positions, thoughts, views and prejudices about how human life and society should best be organised. I don't personally see how any theory (or ideology in this sense) can, or should, claim to be immune from this. Indeed, as Berlin reminds us, those theories or ideologies which do claim to be simply neutral reflections of human interest and rationality are, potentially, the most dangerous.
[229] Particularly in relation to his attempt to distinguish 'liberty' from the

very clearly defined views on the degree of individual liberty each of us is to enjoy, whilst living in political society and on the best means of protecting that liberty. It seems more than a little paradoxical for a school of thought, which actively takes a position on a large number of our political and moral beliefs and on their meanings, and has clearly defined views on the amount of individual liberty each of us is to enjoy in *liberal* society, is completely neutral over the question of 'the good life' and over how it is to be pursued. To put it curtly, it isn't.

In other words, meanings (uses) themselves often carry or sponsor, many such claims of what is 'good', 'true' or 'best', and in a number of ways. Consider the example I discussed in chapter one about Berlin's distinction between liberty and the 'conditions for its exercise', regarding how truly unjustifiable losses of liberty involve a form of human coercion.[230] Yet this alone is enough to affect what is considered to be the good for human beings since, as I said there, it will necessarily have an effect on our moral thinking and moral ordering. This, in other words, will be the degree of freedom allotted, equally, to the human beings living in that society and which they are entitled to claim from the government and from one another. This in turn will have a substantial impact on the kind of life each is able to lead.[231]

Word-use carries a large number of beliefs (and once again, our normative concepts carry something of a privileged status here) regarding, not just the word in question, but also many related matters of belief that affect the way a given speaker, or a given society, chooses to use that word. For example, Berlin thinks that the normal sense of the word freedom in contemporary use is, or should be, that which equates to what he calls 'political freedom', which itself is an analysis tied to a number of other beliefs including, as I say, a given theory of coercion and/or oppression. However, as I pointed out earlier, there are aspects of this analysis (and therefore this application, or use, of the word 'freedom') we should be concerned about. Does freedom of choice suddenly

---

'conditions for its exercise'.
[230] See pp. 16–24 above.
[231] I return to this – vital – point in the conclusion below.

stop being valuable only when the restraint is a human imposition? Clearly not.

Therefore, the meaning of a given normative concept circulating through everyday linguistic communication, will naturally reflect the accumulated ideas, theories, views, beliefs, prejudices and neuroses of the linguistic victors, though to differing degrees in each case. The liberal conception of freedom, as we have seen, reflects the fact that liberals tend to believe in (among other things) the free common market and in representative government and an equality of basic rights, all of which, themselves, reflect further beliefs about such foggy things as 'human nature', the nature of political organisation, 'economic man', the psychology of human motivation, moral belief, and so on. This is why, among other things, Berlin holds the views that he holds on the nature of coercion and its relationship to 'freedom', 'political freedom' and 'economic slavery'. It is all these things – and more – which we don't see beneath, as it were, the surface of language. Use hides many interesting and intricate complexities behind meaning. Language is, to employ what I hope is a useful metaphor, like an iceberg, the tip of which is visible above the surface through contemporary use and application, but a large part of which lies beneath, in the complex and murky depths of meaning and belief. Interestingly, in this way it also mirrors human psychology.[232]

However, by making these observation am I not in danger of making one of the objections which Ronald Dworkin says "need not concern us for long, because they are based on philosophical mistakes"?[233] "Liberalism", Dworkin affirms, "is not self-contradictory: the liberal conception of equality is a principle of political organisation that is required by justice, not a way of life for individuals and liberals as such, are indifferent as to whether people choose to speak out on political matters, or to lead eccentric lives, or otherwise to behave as liberals are supposed to prefer".[234] This however, is not to answer the objection at all, but merely to repeat the formula. Liberals, in fact, are not as indifferent to these matters

---

[232] I discuss this in greater detail in Edge (Forthcoming B).
[233] Dworkin 1978, p. 142.
[234] Dworkin 1978, pp. 142–143.

as they often claim to be. Indeed, they cannot be.

One clue is provided by the word 'equality'.[235] Dworkin's very statement regarding the "liberal conception of equality" itself points to the non-neutrality of the observation. This is a *liberal* interpretation. What is more, it is a liberal interpretation of the concept of equality which will – unavoidably – have implications, major implications in fact, on our pursuit of the good life within liberal society.

Dworkin, in his article on 'Liberalism', conceives of a liberal lawgiver starting afresh in a new society

> Suppose that a liberal is asked to found a new state. He is required to dictate its constitution and fundamental institutions. He must propose a general theory of political distribution, that is, a theory of how whatever the community has to assign, by way of goods, or resources, or opportunities, should be assigned. He will arrive initially at something like the principle of rough equality: resources and opportunities should be distributed, as far as possible, equally, so that roughly the same share of whatever is available is devoted to satisfying the ambitions of each.[236]

This seems a fair principle on which to found a new society, essentially positing that no opportunity is to be denied to one that is not denied to all, and it has, arguably, profoundly radical implications.[237]

However, when it comes to setting up these institutions, they have a rather familiar appearance. The liberal lawgiver

> will then decide that there are no better mechanisms available, as general political institutions, than the two main institutions of our own political economy: the common market, for decisions about what goods shall be produced and how they shall be distributed, and representative democracy, for collective

---

[235] Just as it is by the use of the word 'justice'. Liberals – as Dworkin's next few sentences subtly prove – are not neutral (nor can they be, of course) on the meaning of the word 'justice' and then what is required for it. This, again, will impact substantially on – precisely – what a given society does believe to be the good, or the best, because these will be the conditions ('as required by justice') that will set the parameters for human life and interaction in that society and of course, the reasons for those parameters.
[236] Dworkin 1978, pp. 128–129.
[237] See below.

decisions about what conduct shall be prohibited or regulated so that other conduct might be made possible or convenient. Each of these familiar institutions may be expected to provide a more egalitarian division than any other general arrangement.[238]

Indeed, Dworkin objects to a socialist economy because "the liberal theory of equality rules out that appeal to the inherent value of one theory of what is good in life".[239] This last claim appears somewhat paradoxical. It is immediately clear that these institutions set up by the liberal lawgiver will have (clearly very profound) implications regarding how individuals are able to pursue 'the good life' in liberal society. Dworkin, precisely, thinks that these institutions are 'better' than any other for securing those values and conditions we take as basic to leading a human life over time and that they are necessary for 'justice'. Both choices will, in a very natural and immediate sense, have a profound impact on "the way of life for individuals" Dworkin claims that liberals are neutral on.

This is not to say that Dworkin does not have good reasons for arguing as he does (because, among other things, he believes the market is necessary for equality) but still this does not equate to neutrality.[240] This is because the choice of a capitalist market economy and a representative democracy

---

[238] Dworkin 1978, p. 130. This last statement is, I think, particularly controversial. Is there not a logical case for claiming (what might be considered to be) the contrary here – namely that the most egalitarian solution would be brought about by participatory democracy and a socialist 'economy'? I do not see how a socialist making this response, that greater egalitarian opportunity (and, therefore, greater happiness?) will be better realised under a socialist society and economy, is making any stronger claim regarding what constitutes the 'good life' than Dworkin is by saying that the same principle will best be realised under liberal institutions and representative democracy. Once again, so much depends here on the meaning of certain terms. What conception, for instance, of a socialist economy (should we not be speaking of socialist economies..?), did Dworkin have in mind when he wrote this? What picture of the various 'economies' in question here, comes to the reader's mind as she goes over these statements?

[239] Dworkin 1978, p. 132.

[240] See Dworkin 1981 for his famous argument about this. Dworkin, like Rawls, argues for a liberal world far fairer and far more egalitarian than the one we currently inhabit. See for example, Dworkin 2000, p. 312. It is also worth quoting Stephen Holmes: "no society is liberal as liberals would like" (Holmes 1989, p. 231).

and all that goes with those choices in terms of coercive laws, apparatus and structure, has profound implications for my pursuit of the good over a complete life. For these are the structures which will define human co-operation over time. In terms of the structure I am proposing here, it is not that Dworkin is wrong, any more than he is right, just that these structures have already won out, and won out as 'the best' and/or the most rational. We are not given the choice as to whether we happen to agree or not. And Dworkin's choice (or his liberal lawgiver's choice) is certainly not neutral.

The liberal theory of 'equality' is really no different to the socialistic theory of 'equality' in relation to this question of the 'good life'. It seems to me to be impossible to be neutral regarding this matter, whoever you are. Nor do I understand the need to single "socialism" out here. The argument on behalf of socialism (or the one that interests me) is surely simply that it will provide the most just, the most egalitarian, distribution of resources to enable human beings to live a good life through the pursuit of happiness. There is no division here with liberalism about the need to be neutral regarding the content of what an individual thinks will make her life good, but rather, on the question of what conditions, what alterable conditions, can best secure the opportunity to pursue a good life, through human freedom, for all individuals. Socialism is no more neutral than liberalism about this aspect of the question, but I fail to see how there is any "comprehensive doctrine" here (in Rawls' sense[241]), or any appeal to what is "good in life" (in Dworkin's sense) above or beyond the claims that liberals make. Yet clearly, this doesn't make either alternative neutral – both take a number of positions, and hold to a number of theories, as to how human society can best be ordered to secure those positions and why this should be the case.

In the structure I am proposing, the list of alternatives (whether the alternative is socialism, communism, anarchism, liberalism, conservativism, or something else) is in regard to the questions I began with – which alternative, which collection of alterable human practices, will provide the best arrangements for social co-operation over time through

---

[241] Rawls 1996, p. 13, for example.

distributing bundles (or areas) of individual freedom and, with that, how equal will those bundles be and why? There can be no neutral answers here, as the solution (whatever it happens to be) will have profound effects on the kind of choices we will be free to make and on why we might make those choices (among other things). The best solution will be that which provides the greatest choice-range and to the most equal degree,[242] since this will widen the area of (state) neutrality (so to speak) in the first instance. The greater the realm of negative individual freedom, the greater the choice-range and, *de facto*, the greater the degree of neutrality in relation to those choices (via, amongst other things, an absence of coercive laws). The next step is to show how such arrangements can be rational, sustainable and just, but that is, as I say, the next step. What should not be assumed is that it will automatically be liberalism which provides the best answer and the greatest amount of equal individual liberty in a sustainable way.

Ultimately, any political theorist is trying to argue for the establishment of political, social and economic structures which they believe will best enable human beings to pursue a 'good life'. Liberals argue on behalf of one thing, socialists for another, anarchists for another, and so on because each of these groups takes categorical positions on what constitutes (among other things) 'justice', 'equality' and 'freedom'. That however, means taking a number of other positions on how human beings are going to interact with one another, over a complete life, in the various polities these different groups are advocating for. I don't believe that they can, or should, lay claim to neutrality just because each can, and should, lay claim to neutrality on what Rawls calls 'comprehensive doctrines' of morality and/or religion.[243] However, just because they might be netural on these questions of a more comprehensive order, still they cannot be neutral on their answers to those fundamental questions of political philosophy (and many other questions), which will necessarily have an impact on the 'way of life for individuals', because that life will be defined (both restricted and, in the negative sense, liberated) by the laws required by (any given thinker's or group's) conception of 'justice'.

---

[242] See the conclusion below.
[243] See, for example, Rawls 1996, xviii ff.

On another related matter, it is unclear what picture of socialistic society Dworkin has in his mind here. He seems to be thinking of some notion of socialism, within which individuals are compelled to sacrifice their own self-interest and their own pursuit of the good in favour of the common interest or good. Goals in this story are collective, not individual. However, if this (or something similar) is what Dworkin has in mind, it is in itself a caricature of socialistic socio-political organisation and the socialistic conception of equality, at least as I construe socialism and socialistic goals, though there are, of course, multiple socialisms.

Though Dworkin (or any other liberal) would be entitled to reply – 'that's your problem! I have very good reasons for looking at socialism the way I do as its history has proved to be anything but promising, especially to individual freedom. It's down to *you* to show us otherwise.'

So this places (as I have been suggesting throughout) the onus on those of us who do happen to think that a given set of alterable human practices, which differ from the present set in a number of ways, will provide the best and/or the most just solutions to the questions I began with. What is required here, in other words, is an account of this negative individual freedom under the different sets of alterable human practices, whichever set a given writer happens to ascribe to.

Look at it this way. A socialistic account of equal liberty, which I will outline my own version of in part two of this project, might be thought to be beneficial to individual liberty, and therefore, the content-neutral pursuit of the good life, for a number of reasons. Firstly, there is a common stock of all goods (with possible minor aesthetic exceptions which all might agree to, such as heirlooms, keepsakes and the like) available for all to use. As G.A. Cohen puts it in a famous example, communal property relations give me access to Mr Morgan's yacht, an access I would not otherwise have within a private property system,[244] though, note again, as I mentioned earlier, how this requires a theory of human labour, resources and productivity.

Secondly, an equal access to changed educational structures gives each individual greater access to those tools which can

---

[244] See Cohen 1979, pp. 11–12.

best enable her to develop freely as an individual.[245] Once again there must be a theory attached to this, but the basic point is that egalitarian educational arrangements (which involve a vastly altered educational structure from the one we currently have) allow each individual, without any exception, to develop in accordance with the natural dictates of her character, abilities and emotions. This period of our development, where we first encounter and develop skills that we are able to use during our continuing pursuit of the good life, is crucial to individual liberty. The more I learn, the more opportunities and skills (and so on) I have access to as I grow up, the greater the choices that are available to me as I reach adulthood. This society might make reference to a theory based around the 'communalisation of opportunities'[246] to establish equal individual liberty and it is immediately clear that, for such a theory to be successful, it would have to confront a large number of issues in detail. The key here is a theory which combats the vastly unequal educational structures and access to them, which exist even in wealthy nations, let alone when the analysis is expanded to include less fortunate parts of the world.

Thirdly, under such a system, government would be run according to the principles of participatory democracy, that is by you and me, and everyone else, together in neighbourhood and workplace assembly. We would, therefore, have increased liberty to vote, to walk to, and speak in, political assembly (whether physical, in local stadia and the like, or virtual), and to propose measures before our fellow citizens. Again, the Athenian democratic insight is valuable here. This is not a system designed to give power to all so that they can wield it with an iron fist, but the opposite of this – to prevent others from doing the same to us, from imposing a social, political and economic structure upon us in the first place. It is about the *absence* of coercion in the simple negative sense.[247] This is not about imposing a concrete and constricted way of life on others, but, on the contrary, to prevent them doing the same to us. The Athenians remind us that, rather than restricting

---

[245] See Edge (Forthcoming D).
[246] See also pp. 24–29 above.
[247] See Edge 2009, especially pp. 34 ff.

and limiting it, we, the people, might prefer a vastly expanded realm of individual liberty than that which is allowed us by our representatives. But readers will already have guessed what I am going to say next – yet further theories, or accounts, are needed here, particularly regarding (as I have mentioned before) rights and the rule of law. I will try to meet this possible objection – that we, the collective people, would simply seek to ride roughshod over what are now called individual rights – shortly.

This system, though I have given only the most cursory illustration of it, is far from providing a single theory of, or answer to, 'what is good in life'. To the contrary, I would argue on its behalf, or on behalf of a similar socialism that sought to make opportunities to pursue a genuinely free and happy life equal, because it provides better conditions for all to pursue whatever it is that each believes to be the 'good life' than those available under free-market capitalism. It is, therefore, to be viewed as being better able to realise basic liberal values[248] than those solutions liberals themselves put forward.

The argument is not, in other words, that it is rational for human beings to put the collective interest before individual interest, and that it is in the best interests of human beings to subsume individual well-being to that of the social body. It is simply that, as individuals, we will fare better, in terms of our equal individual liberty, under egalitarian equal liberty, than under structures which form a common market, regulated by financial exchange and by representative government. Further, the argument also claims that the alterable set of structures under egalitarian equal liberty will be more 'just', but for no deeper reason that that sought by liberals. It will only be more just, in other words, because it equalises opportunities to pursue happiness through individual freedom, whilst living in human society over time. Our starting point is the same, in other words, as liberalism, it is just the result which is different. I will try to say more about this in a moment.

---

[248] E.g., Holmes 1995, p. 16: "We can say that the highest political values, from a liberal perspective, are psychological security and personal independence for all, legal impartiality within a single system of laws applied equally to all, the human diversity fostered by liberty, and collective self-rule through elected government and uncensored discussion."

This, then, is a fundamentally Berlinean point. "Even if," as Berlin says, "no hard and fast rule can be provided, it still remains the case that the measure of the liberty of a man or a group is, to a large degree, determined by the range of choosable possibilities."[249] The account of this socio-political order to come in part two, then, argues that this socialistic form of life, far from being a comprehensive, quasi-religious doctrine, on the kind of life that will finally set human beings free in some higher sense, would, on the contrary, simply seek to increase the range of choosable possibilities and options and make them equally accessible and available to all.

Now, I am not trying to do the opposite of what I have been arguing on behalf of throughout. I am not, in other words, prejudging the issue. When given the free choice to do so, we may decide to adopt this new system (as I would, I am happy to admit, urge us to do), but equally, we may not. I am not arguing that this is the only rational choice for us to make, according to my own subjective view of human nature, or economic and social development (or whatever else I may happen to believe), and that, because of this, if you vote against it you are wrong to do so and, therefore, I, understanding human rationality correctly, am perfectly justified in coercing you to accept after all, since this (and only this) will give you 'true liberty'.

Rather than arguing this – the route, indeed, of positive liberty doctrines – I am making no statement on what I think human rationality actually is. That it is decided by the process, by me, perhaps, but only alongside you. I am only outlining what *I* think is the best and the fairest (and this is a separate issue, more on which shortly) means of ordering social co-operation. But you, together with everyone else, are free to disagree. I am also urging others, including liberals, to put forward their views of what they think the best and the fairest means of social cooperation to be, how it would work, and why. Just as, indeed, Rawls has done, at least partly. We then decide from the list of alternatives.

What I am suggesting is that 'positive liberty' doctrines, similar to the one I have just outlined, can be found in unexpected places. The theory of liberty I am constructing is an

---

[249] Berlin 2002c, p. 272.

attempt to provide a way out of this problem. Nor, of course, is this a neutral intervention on behalf of the structure(s) necessary for human beings to pursue their own conceptions of the good over a complete life. I might argue, in part two, that we would do better under such a system, in this regard, than under liberalism, but this doesn't render my claims neutral. Just like Dworkin, I am simply trying to advocate the best *means* for human beings to realise their individual ends. What, however, we must recognise is that those ends are (in matters of political, social and economic structures) inseparable from the means under which they are pursued. The structure I describe does not tell human beings what their individual chosen ends should be, it merely argues that we will be better off pursuing them under these alterable structures than under liberal ones, since this society might actually (as it happens) enable the realisation of certain values (such as liberty and peace) central to liberal, and to human, thought better than liberal societies tend to do. But it is for you to decide whether or not you agree.

Political Theory and Positive Liberty

Before moving on, let me just sum up so far. I am proposing a structure (starting from *now*) wherein the answering of the fundamental questions of political philosophy is left – empirically and actually, in the real world, here and now – to you and me and everyone else together. This is the participatory structure whereby we decide, you and me, what it is in our best interests to want from a form of socio-political organisation and, indeed, why. This means that these vital political issues and institutions will not be decided on our behalf (as they traditionally have been) according to some subjective views on (such things as) what it is our best interest to want, what it is most rational, and most moral, for us to do, how politics should be done and by whom, human motivation, human nature and the psychological structure of humanity, among other things, beliefs and views themselves tied to further beliefs, thoughts, prejudices and neuroses about many related matters and things.

On top of this (so to speak) stands the linguistic and epistemological structure I have proposed which recognises that

– mainly owing to the structure of language and the means by which we acquire certain aspects of it – this task is, as we stand here today, neither going to be easy, nor 'free', and I am proposing a structure to tackle that. If both of these structures are followed, this then helps us to tackle the problems raised in Berlin's important account of the dangers of positive liberty doctrines.

This theory also, then, seeks to avoid some of the defects (as I see them) of Rawls' *Theory of Justice* and the works which followed it. However, as I have said, the starting points are fundamentally the same. Rawls sets the questions as well as the standard. Rawls attempted to find a political conception of justice that could be adopted by (or that could be acceptable to) all the members of a modern, cosmopolitan, democracy who each possessed conflicting interpretations of the good.[250] He attempted to work out, through a number of ingenious devices, the fairest terms of social co-operation for human beings living in society over time. 'Justice as Fairness', Rawls' solution, is *political* because it claims to take no stand on what constitutes 'the good life'. In a modern democratic society – based fundamentally on pluralism – citizens do not share the same views regarding what constitutes 'the good' and, therefore, it is necessary to find a political conception of justice, that all could agree to, which remains neutral on this question of the good and only specifies the fairest means of social co-operation over time, under which citizens can autonomously pursue their own conceptions of the good over a complete life.

The structure I am suggesting here, then, attempts to do, in many essentials, the same thing. It aims, in other words, to discover those conditions that can realise a structure through which each and every individual is able to best pursue his or her own conception of the good (in society over time). The difference is, of course, that this is not an 'otherworldly', 'ahistorical', device of representation,[251] but an actual appeal on behalf of changes in material human conditions (in particular linguistic communication) to bring about the kind

---

[250] See, for example, Rawls 1996, pp. xviii, xli, xlvii, etc.
[251] Rawls himself, of course, openly acknowledged and celebrated this aspect of his theory. See, for example, Rawls 1996, p. lxii; Rawls 2001, pp. 16–17.

of free-choice situation I have described, where each of us, does indeed choose, from a number of competing alternatives, those structures that we believe will be most conducive to promoting the values we hold as key to our individual, autonomous, pursuit of the good over a complete life. Far from employing, a 'veil of ignorance',[252] my theory, instead, celebrates the fact that each and every individual brings his or her own personality to the empirical party. There is a kind of veil of ignorance, but it works in a different, and natural, way.

For instance, if each of us approached this task with the same information on the available systems, as free and equal citizens (or inhabitants), would we, when faced with the choice between an equal system (similar to the one I describe in part two) and an unequal one (similar to free-market capitalism, for example), go for the unequal one and accept the inequalities? Would it be rational for us to do so? In other words, if I did not know how things were going to turn out, if, say, I had a 50% chance of being among the disadvantaged, would I go for this option? Or would I go for the egalitarian one?[253] Under Rawls' plan, the answer (or part of it, at least[254]) has already been provided for us because Rawls himself claims to know what it would be rational for us to do.

Rawls rejects the idea of a wide guarantee of the fair value for all the basic liberties, "if that guarantee means that income and wealth are to be distributed equally, it is irrational: it does not allow society to meet the requirements of social organisation and efficiency."[255] Or, as Rawls puts it elsewhere,

---

[252] For a full explanation of this idea (and its undoubted benefits, at least for a theory such as Rawls'), see, for example, Rawls 1999a, pp. 118–123; Rawls 2001, pp. 80 ff.

[253] As Rawls himself acknowledges (see below), I would go for the egalitarian one. His further claim is that this condition does not necessarily need to apply to society following the original position. "If there are inequalities in income and wealth, and differences in authority and degrees of responsibility, that work to make everyone better off in comparison with the benchmark of equality, why not permit them?" Rawls 1999a, pp. 130–131. Cf., a plausible objection to this in n. 257 below.

[254] I fully accept that Rawls leaves the question of whether the means of production are to be communally, or privately, owned for the next stage in the process (which he, quite deliberately, does not provide). See Rawls 2001, § 32. 6 pp. 114–115.

[255] Rawls 2001, § 46. 1 p. 151.

since one might also think that the requirements of citizens as free and equal moral persons are equal, why is not an equal share of *all* primary goods the sole principle of justice? I cannot argue this question here and shall only comment that, although the parties in the original position know that the persons they represent require primary goods, it does not follow that it is rational for the parties as their representatives to agree to such a strict principle of equality. The two principles of justice regulate social and economic inequalities in the basic structure so that these inequalities work over time to the greatest benefit to the least advantaged citizens. *These principles express a more rational agreement*".[256]

"A political conception of justice," Rawls explains, "must take into account the requirements of social organisation and economic efficiency. The parties would accept inequalities in income and wealth when these work effectively to improve everyone's situation starting from an equal division."[257]

One of the problems with this is that it is doing exactly what I have cautioned against us doing. It ascribes to a subjective view of economic theory and organisation (an egalitarian system *could* be more efficient[258]) as well as to a subjective view of human nature, including (perhaps implicitly) human motivation, human labour and psychology. I mean by this last comment that, when we (or those who are representing us, in Rawls' account) approach the original position as individual human beings, efficiency might well not, psychologically and emotionally, be all that we're about. Equally, 'efficiency' in the production of what? Wealth, social freedom, happiness, conditions under which the 'good' can be pursued individually, or something else? For this in effect, begs a number of questions. What is the primary goal

---

[256] Rawls 1982, p. 173 (my italics).
[257] Rawls 2001, § 36. 2 p. 123. Cf. n. 253 above. This expresses the second principle of justice which asserts that inequalities "are to be to the greatest benefit of the least-advantaged members of society", Rawls 2001, § 13. 1 pp. 42-43. Cf. Rawls 1999a, pp. 130–139. The problem is that this principle is impossible to measure without empirical data measuring how individuals living under the different forms of social organisation do, in fact, fare comparatively. There are also the objections I raise above.
[258] Or, more importantly, it could do better regarding what the 'efficiency' is fundamentally designed to produce or achieve, i.e. individual liberty and human happiness and well-being.

of human 'efficiency'? Should it simply be the production of wealth or, instead, the expansion of the realm of human freedom, for the two are not necessarily one and the same, especially in unequal societies such as ours. Surely the aim of efficiency in social productivity is to create, expand and protect conditions of social co-operation in which human life can best flourish through individual freedom. Yet clearly, this is not necessarily synonymous with the production of wealth and efficiency in monetary exchange.

Of course, if Rawls has in mind those (totalitarian) pictures of socialism I have mentioned during the course of my discussion, it is, as I have said, hardly surprising that his individuals would not opt for the more exacting, egalitarian, option.[259] Such pictures are not uncommon in the analyses of liberal writers. Matthew Kramer, in the course of denouncing Marxism as a positive liberty doctrine, describes "the wickedness of Marxist regimes" as "incoherent", "pernicious", "fanciful … unintelligible", "repulsive" and "hideous utopian folly" in little over a paragraph.[260] Of course, it would not be rational for us to endorse, or accept, such a ("Marxist") picture, and this is exactly the response that Kramer is trying to achieve in the minds of his readers.[261] Yet, as I have said, there are other ways to approach socialistic ideas and systems – as I have been suggesting, socialistic systems might actually be able to realise liberal values better than liberal systems do.

Further, Stephen Holmes reminds us that

> while liberals have a better grasp of economic realities than socialists and communists, the most obvious superiority of liberal over Marxist thought stems from liberalism's persistent concern for – and Marxism's infamous blindness to – abuses of accumulated power.[262]

This insight into economic realities enables him to say that "only a vigorous market economy, relying on individual incentives, can produce a surplus worth distributing by

---

[259] Which he clearly does – see, for example, Rawls 2001, § 41.4 p. 138.
[260] Kramer 2003, pp. 159–160.
[261] Again, note Wittgenstein 2001, § 23 p. 10, and (famously) Austin 1962, on all the different ways in which language can be employed to question, to warn (as here), to state, to ask, to think, to judge, and so on.
[262] Holmes 1995, p. 18.

political means."[263] That is some claim, but it cannot be the simple statement of the facts it purports to be. There may well, in fact, be very good reasons for believing the contrary, and the current conditions of global capitalism clearly suggest that the evidence for Holmes' view is not straightforward.

Kwasi Wiredu, in an illuminating discussion of traditional African thought, suggests that

> the principles underlying the choices of a communistic culture, however, is not only compatible with the golden rule [of morality] but also analogous to it. Individuals in such cultures are enjoined to think in terms not of what they can gain from their society, but what society can gain from them, so, however, that all can prosper.[264]

No man is a palm tree, as the Akans say.[265]

Liberals might say that this is the true face of communalism revealed – that individuals under communalism are forced to abdicate their individualism, and their individual goals, in favour of the needs of the collectivity. Here, they will say, is proof that communalism does indeed endorse a single conception of 'what is good in life', rather than allowing individuals to live how they think best. Yet this is clearly not what Wiredu is saying here. The Akan suggestion is that individuals will fare better, will prosper, the more they look to the well-being of the collective – if everyone prospers, then so do you. Liberals perhaps think the opposite (and certainly free market capitalism does). But this brings out the linguistic battle nicely. The Akan (and other communalistic cultures) may be wrong, or liberals may be wrong. But, it would be paradoxical to suggest that either is neutral on the matter. These are simply different arguments related to the highly important matter of how individual human beings (living in society) will best prosper.

The point is not that Wiredu is right any more than that he is wrong, but if we accept such statements as those I have just cited as neutral expressions of the truth, or of the facts,

---

[263] Holmes 1995, p. 36.
[264] Wiredu 2001, p. 173.
[265] For more on the implications of this saying, and its relevance to communalistic society and human well-being, see Wiredu 1996, part IV.

we will, necessarily, be closing ourselves off from alternative modes of thought, under the accounts of which we might actually fare better as individuals and as a species. Once again, the language-picture we have inherited, with all its accumulated dogmas relating to 'human nature', 'rationality', 'efficiency', 'political organisation' and so on, takes on the appearance of a positive liberty doctrine. Such subjectively-held theories are inherently tied to what a society, nation or body of thought believes to be, and expects from, 'liberty'.

These kind of dogmas circulate everywhere, and often in unexpected places. Take one example from "the most eloquent of all defenders of freedom and privacy",[266] Benjamin Constant. Constant, to judge by his use of language, was pretty certain that he had discovered what it was that we, the moderns, desired, and what would enable us to be free. "Called as we are", Constant said, "by our happy revolution ... to enjoy the benefits of representative government, the *only one* in the shelter of which we could find some freedom and peace today".[267] Constant goes on to tell the moderns exactly the kind of freedom they (we) desire.

> It follows from what I have just indicated that we can no longer enjoy the liberty of the ancients, which consisted in an active and constant participation in collective power. Our freedom *must* consist (*doit se composer*) of peaceful enjoyment and private independence.[268]

He is no less certain later on, adding in the middle of his lecture that, "individual independence is the first need of the moderns: consequently one must never require from them any sacrifices to establish political liberty".[269]

He writes elsewhere,

> Notice that the necessary aim of those without property is to obtain some: all the means which you grant them are sure to be used for this purpose. If, to the freedom to use their talents and industry, which you owe them, you add political rights which

---

[266] Berlin 2002b, p. 173.
[267] Constant 1988b, p. 314 (trans. Fontana. My italics).
[268] Constant 1988b, p. 316 (trans. Fontana. My italics). See also Constant 1988a, p. 104.
[269] Constant 1988b, p. 321 (trans. Fontana).

you do not owe them, these rights, in the hands of the greatest number, will inevitably serve to encroach upon property. They will pursue it by this irregular course instead of following the natural one: labour. It will become, for them, a source of corruption, for the state a source of disorder."[270]

I don't think it is unreasonable to suggest that the words "irregular" and "natural" here could have similar effects to the division between the "higher" and the "lower" self discussed above.[271]

These statements can hardly be said to be neutral regarding what constitutes the good life and the means by which to pursue it. It could be argued that arguments like this were responsible, and remain responsible, for horrendous forms of exploitation and brutal conditions in the labour market, leading to physical injury, mental distress, exhaustion and early death. For it is "natural", the true aim and goal of humanity, if we aim to avoid 'corruption', to fight our own way up the social ladder to secure our own property, no matter the barriers, the size of the struggle in our own way. It was just this kind of argument about which Berlin was (rightly) so worried[272] and it is just this kind of claim which hides, beneath the surface of meaning,[273] behind the contemporary use of normative concepts and ideas in our inherited language-picture.

It is not hard to find similar examples elsewhere. To return to Rawls again, he claims, for example, that "any modern society, even a well-ordered one, must rely on some inequalities to be well designed and effectively organised".[274] Yet this statement of fact, can be no more true than his earlier statement (quoting Robert Dahl approvingly) that, "today no unit smaller than a country can provide the conditions necessary for a good life".[275] He adds in a very Constantean vein,

---

[270] Constant 1988c, p. 215.
[271] See, in particular, pp. 36–40 above.
[272] See, especially, the quotation on p. 37 above.
[273] See p. 74 above.
[274] Rawls 2001, § 16. 1 p. 55. This claim must largely depend upon what Rawls exactly means by "inequalities" (as well as by the terms "well designed" and "effectively organised"), which is unclear.
[275] Rawls 2001, n. 12 p. 13.

> Justice as Fairness agrees with the strand of the liberal tradition (represented by Constant and Berlin) that regards the equal political liberties (the liberties of the ancients) as having in general less intrinsic value than, say, freedom of thought and liberty of conscience (the liberties of the moderns). By this is meant, among other things, that in a modern democratic society, taking a continuing and active part in public life generally has, and may indeed reasonably have, a lesser place in the conceptions of the (complete) good of most citizens. In a modern democratic society politics is not the focus of life as it was for native born male citizens in the Athenian city state.[276]

But when, for example, have we ever given our opinion on this matter and, what is more, given it freely? How does Rawls know that "we" don't value such participatory freedoms? Our social world is simply not set up to allow us to explore democratic, Athenian-style, participation, or even, generally speaking, to think about and decide whether or not we might want to explore such a political system, though it might have potential benefits (as well as potential defects), particularly around human empowerment and self-confidence and, as I have said, around an expanded area for free movement itself.

There are, in fact, very few grounds for Rawls' claim. Most of us have never been asked, or even thought about, what we might think about the Athenian-style 'political liberties'. I cannot see how these claims can represent taking a neutral position on what constitutes the 'good life'. Liberals, no less than socialists, conservatives, or any other group they attack in relation to this claim,[277] have no problem in telling us where the good life, or certain conditions required for it, is, or are, to be found. Their claims are not rendered neutral simply by the fact that we live under liberal institutions.

All this can have an effect not a little unlike that Berlin saw as being at the heart of the positive concept of liberty. In other words, through the very simple and natural processes by which we acquire language and knowledge, we can be led into thinking that the world we inhabit is unquestionably the

---
[276] Rawls 2001, § 43. 3 p. 143.
[277] See especially Dworkin 1978.

right one, the truly rational and most harmonious one, for us, that those who came before us found the right answers as to what was best for us (as members of a particular nation, participants in a particular culture or religion, individuals who inhabit a particular moment of historical time, and so on), that our social, political and economic structures provide us with 'freedom'. Our predecessors have found 'true equality', 'true liberty', that form of social, political and economic organisation which will best allow us to develop 'true happiness', that is 'most rational', 'most efficient', and so on.

This, then, goes back, once again to Quine's Martha/Tom example and the issues around it. It is this language-picture we come to internalise, together with all its accompanying and questionable assumptions, prejudices, beliefs and views about political society and social and economic conditions. As I have said, there will very likely be a fair amount of evidence to suggest that such claims might (in part, at least) be true, or accurate, but there is also likely to be a fair amount of evidence to suggest the contrary and which might enable us to question some of these basic beliefs and assumptions.

The example does not have to be pressed so far that we end up comparing our societies to Hitler's Germany, Franco's Spain, Stalin's Russia or Mussolini's Italy (for example). There is enough conflict, exploitation, death and suffering, even on the streets of so-called prosperous nations, let alone when the picture is expanded, as it should be, to include all the peoples of the earth, to make us question these arrangements, and the judgements which lie behind them. Is free-market capitalism the "only" means of securing the kind of social productivity necessary for humans to flourish? Is nation-state, globalised, capitalism the most rational form of arrangement for us to accept? Are wide inequalities in the basic structure rational, and will they always be so? Is the good-life only possible in territories the size of nation-states governed by representatives? These are not neutral matters and how they are answered will clearly have a significant bearing on the way human life, on the pursuit of happiness over a complete life in conditions of sustainable social cooperation, will endure and flourish. In short, do these conditions and structures, these alterable human practices, enable us (and I do mean us) to be free, or are there different ways and means of organising human co-operation which will enable us to be freer and to enjoy that freedom in more equal measure?

If we are to take Berlin's argument seriously, then we need to be freed from the kind of assumptions, beliefs, thoughts, theories, views, prejudices and neuroses which make-up our accumulated language-picture so we can all together (if you can forgive the phrase) judge those judgements. There is no completely neutral, impartial, reflection of human rationality and human need harmlessly contained in our language-picture, nor is there any other one waiting to be found in any other 'conceptual scheme' or language-picture. If we can be freed from this assumption, freed from the dangerous idea that ideology has been vanquished, or that it ever could be, we might then find ourselves freer to judge human freedom in the first place. As Berlin himself so eloquently put it, "few governments, it has been observed, have found much difficulty in causing their subjects to generate any will that the government wanted. The triumph of despotism is to force the slaves to declare themselves free."[278] We may not be slaves, but we should, at the very least, begin to wonder how free we actually are and, with that, how much more freedom might, for us, be humanly possible.

The Naturalisation of Political Philosophy

Thoughts, Davidson reminds us, must have a history. I am suggesting that this simple acknowledgement, and the basic implications which follow from it, has profound consequences for political philosophy and for the type of political philosophy we should be doing. By this I mean that we should be focusing on our language-picture and the uses and applications of our normative concepts it carries, why it carries those particular meanings (uses),[279] and at all the judgements that lie behind them. This also means targeting our linguistic interventions, as political philosophers, at the basic Davidsonian triangle of two minds interpreting a shared and common world, that is,

---

[278] Berlin 2002b, pp. 210–211.
[279] I.E. by looking at the specific series of historical linguistic battles which have got us to this (semantic) point.

everyone and the world that surrounds us. We are the ones left free (in two senses) to judge our political language and our political world.

The word "free" has an important role to play. I have in mind here a much more demanding, or exacting, idea of 'freedom of thought' than the somewhat impoverished one circulating in everyday political and moral discourse (meaning: something like my liberty to believe what I want without fear of coercion by others). Freedom of thought certainly means what is contained in these last parentheses, but it also seems to imply something more. The degree of physical freedom I enjoy is defined by the width of the area left to me by the coercive laws (and morality) of my society (or even of my species), the number of doors open to me, the number of paths available to me to walk down. Is the case any different mentally speaking? The freedom of the mental is defined in just the same way, by the number of mental opportunities available to me, and these opportunities can be closed off, or hindered, or destroyed, by a number of factors, including fear and the context of rationality within which each of us lives and thinks. I cannot walk through doors, or down paths, I do not know are there, just as I cannot freely walk through doors which I believe stand in the way of my meeting with a dragon, or a murderer who is after me, because I know, or have been told, or have assumed, that this is what is waiting for me behind those doors. Or, to put it a better way, I cannot walk through doors I do not know are there, just as I cannot freely walk through doors it would simply not be rational for me to walk through. There are some further very interesting implications here around our political and moral language, rationality, assumption and judgement, related to these kinds of issues, and the kinds of language-use, I have just been discussing. This is where the process of 'naturalisation' comes in. But what might be the implications of this?

The first part is, as I have attempted to sketch, via an account of first-person authority, placing the answering of the fundamental questions of political philosophy (as I, following Rawls, have construed them to be) into our own hands. The second part concerns giving us the tools to answer them to the best of our abilities and as freely as possible, meaning providing us with the largest amount of (genuine, realisable and rational) choice. It might be objected that this is doomed to failure because ideology, prejudice and subjective theory will always get in the way, but this is not enough to prevent us from trying. It can be no legitimate argument against a different theory, or system, that it doesn't get us to utopia, even though it may be (and, in this case, I must hold the view that it is) better than what we have now.

So, finally, what might all this mean in practice? Firstly, giving each of us far better access to our moral and political concepts as we grow up, so that we learn to think about them as a vital part of our universe, no less important, it could be argued, than the movement of the planets, the state of the environment, how our bodies work, and so on. It should be an important part of our schooling and education for us to learn about freedom, about justice, about equality, about peace (together with our other normative concepts), about the ways in which we are free, just, equal, and peaceful and the ways we might hope to be freer, more just, more equal and more peaceful. And this observation must hold, if it needed saying, for whatever form of society and social organisation we happen to find ourselves in. This should be a basic part of our confronting, through language, the world we come to inhabit as we grow older. Once again, this raises problems, particularly around whether, as I mentioned earlier, our governments will freely concede tools to potentially help their people replace them with (potentially) something better, but I shall come back to this.

Secondly, that we be given far greater access to alternative modes of thought during this reconfigured learning process, helping us to consider the different ways we can become more just, more free and so on and, equally, different ways of considering the ongoing human project in general. This means access, not only to such devices as the 'spectrum of liberty',[280] through which I have elsewhere looked at long-forgotten ways of thinking about our shared political world from – loosely – within our own traditions, but, possibly much more importantly, to the rich variety of thought beyond those traditions within (so-called) 'alien' traditions. I am

---

[280] Cf. Edge (Forthcoming B).

thinking of alternative ways of looking at political and ethical thinking from across the globe, such as those offered by Kwasi Wiredu,[281] Thaddeus Metz[282] and Mahatma Gandhi,[283] to make an arbitrary selection. These are just three highly interesting examples from a globe of interesting traditions reflecting different ways of looking at how human beings can most successfully live together, ranging from the Western traditions which we have most contact with, to the different schools of thought in Islam, Buddhism, Africa, the Middle East and the Far East, to, again, give a brief and arbitrary example.[284] It is not that any one of these traditions, any more than our own, will provide the final answer, or the true conceptual scheme, but our dialogue, our range for thought and, therefore, our mental freedom, will be hugely improved and increased the more we have contact with ways of thinking about the ethical and the political which differ from, and challenge, our own. As Davidson says, "what is certain is that the clarity and effectiveness of our concepts grows with the growth of our understanding of others. There are no definite limits to how far dialogue can or will take us."[285]

Thirdly, we must investigate our language-picture to try to help to detach our own subjective theories or prejudices (on a variety of issues) from our moral and political concepts when we come to undertake the task. We might, for instance, as the examples I have mentioned show, adhere to a particular conception of 'liberty' (which we call, or believe to be, 'true liberty') because we have certain settled views on (say) 'human nature', the nature of political society, 'economic man', technological development and so on. Yet, as Berlin himself recognised, liberty is liberty, justice is justice, equality is equality, and fairness is fairness (and so on). We will not get very far unless we start confronting these concepts on their own terms. If we are (for example) constructing an

---

[281] See Wiredu 1996, 2001, for example.
[282] Metz 2007 presents a fascinating overview of (sub-Saharan) African moral philosophy and, in particular, the concept of *ubuntu*, which might be usefully compared with Western schools of moral thought. As Davidson says (see above), there are no limits as to how far dialogue and communication will take us. See also Cartledge and Edge 2009.
[283] See, especially, Gandhi 1997.
[284] See Goody 2007 for a similar idea.
[285] Davidson 2001b, p. 219.

analysis of freedom, then we need to start with freedom itself and how we can construct social worlds which will increase the amount of human freedom for all. This means looking at those "alterable human practices", at "what I could otherwise do", and understanding all the many ways, with the world as it currently now is, in which individual freedom is restrained, constrained, hindered and downright annihilated and which are not always the result of deliberate, or intentional, human practices. We must first think of how any given social world can best promote human freedom.

Fourthly, we must turn, finally, to the doors available to us to open and the paths available to us to walk down. To enable us to approach all of the doors, the opportunities, the total spectrum of potential choices, openly and freely, we must be able to approach those choices with an open mind and without prejudice. We must be able to see those choices for what they really are and not some bastardised caricature of their essential structure. This is fundamentally, a point about rationality. Some, probably many, are not, for example, wholly free to approach the door behind which the socialist dragon is lurking, simply because they have a tendency to believe that it is a lurking dragon, in other words, a totalitarian and monstrous form of social organisation, which gives no thought to individual needs, wishes and interests because it is so absorbed in the pursuit of the common and collective good. 'Look', the thought might run, 'at the history of socialism, it does not represent a promising choice, it cannot be a rational choice for me, a rational human being, to approach that door.' The same might well go for other theories of social organisation, anarchism, communism, anarcho-syndicalism, participatory democracy and all the various conceptions of these that differ from one another in a number of regards. Each is attached, in a number of ways, to a number of deeply rooted beliefs which are prejudicial to the realisation of those systems in practice.[286]

---

[286] For example, participatory democracy is often thought to be naturally inimical to the separation of powers, the rule of law and individual liberty. For a challenge to these views in more detail, see Edge 2009; Cartledge and Edge 2009. A common objection to anarchist ideas, to take another example, is that 'human nature' (viewed in this instance as essentially morally depraved) would not sustain a lack of social organisation, including the

It will be, then, the task of those who adhere to different systems of social, political and economic organisation, to produce a picture of them which will be acceptable to rational human beings. It is not merely enough, in other words, to lift the present system 'into the full light of day', but it is just as necessary to produce a reasonable and workable picture of the new world for each of us to judge freely.

These, then, are the kinds of things we will need to think about if we are to approach the structure I am proposing, whereby each of us debates, discusses and ultimately chooses the form of social organisation we wish to live under. As I say, this process starts from *now*, since, regardless of the problems I will shortly turn to, nothing, or no one, can actually prevent us from undertaking it, since we (or some of us) are fortunate to live in nations which offer freedom of speech to their inhabitants and citizens.

In many ways, this is simply laying bare what political philosophy tries to do anyway – the problems begin to arise when we start to think about whether the process you and I are (hopefully) beginning now can be extended to everyone else, how and when? It seems appropriate to start considering some of these problems now.

(Some) Problems

Before concluding this first part of my project, I wish to answer a few possible objections. Of course, I'm sure readers will pose further questions and equally, may not be satisfied with my own pre-emptive strikes. Furthermore, a number of responses to (possible) objections will have to wait until the appearance of part two. I suspect one major objection will be that the system of 'egalitarian equal liberty' I have briefly mentioned will not work in practice, but that is something I will have to respond to throughout my analysis in part two of this project. So these cursory remarks will have to do for the time being.

---

absence of what we now call the 'state'. It could be countered that this is far too pessimistic a view of human nature and represents little more than a subjective prejudice. Kropotkin 1995 presents a lively and genuine challenge to this kind of view, though it is not my purpose here to enter into the unending dispute over human capacity to do good, and human capacity to do evil. I will return to this in Edge (Forthcoming C).

I have already mentioned the problem of whether or not the structure I am proposing here in part one could ever actually be a concrete structure, a kind of referendum on human freedom, peace and justice, contributed to by liberals, socialists, conservatives, communists, anarchists, participatory democrats and others. It is highly unlikely that our governments will readily relinquish their power to this kind of debate, even if such a concrete structure would (from my perspective at least) be the most desirable outcome.

However, this does not signal the end for the project. Not only does this point not deal with my argument (it is about practicalities), no one can stop us from engaging in the debate because we are fortunate enough to live under conditions of free speech and free association – if we happen to live in one of the 'prosperous democracies' and, indeed, in certain other parts of the world.

Yet, this clearly opens up the proverbial can of worms all of its own. For, since the project ultimately aims at global peace, I am just as concerned (if not more so) with human beings who do not inhabit the territories of those democracies. These remarks impact hugely on an author's place in his or her world and it is an uncomfortable feeling. For it should make us question *how* we reach people. If so brilliant and influential an author as Quentin Skinner can question the impact of his own project on public life,[287] what hope do the rest of us have? This is not me being simply self-effacing, since these represent vital and genuine questions for a project such as the one I have outlined. Skinner's work has been translated into more than twenty languages at the last count,[288] and his influence as an academic (and beyond) is palpable, if not quantifiable. Although, once again, these points do not settle the *argument*, they are still problems and problems, ultimately, it will be left to history and us to solve.

Furthermore, it is not just vested interests of the kind I have mentioned which we would need to overcome, but the accessibility of a text itself is of huge importance. Once again, I cannot comment on this, but if my argument about

---

[287] Skinner 2005. See n. 184 above.
[288] See the back sleeve to Skinner 2008a.

the naturalisation of political philosophy (and ethics[289]) is accepted, this should certainly mean that we need to question how we, who believe in socio-political change, reach wide audiences and moreover, audiences who do not necessarily speak our own language. And further, how those audiences reach *us*.[290] Davidson is surely right that communication with others will refine our own understanding of our place within the world[291] and this has radical implications. These are wide, but also interesting, problems. We write to reach people, but are we writing in the right way to reach people?

As George Orwell wrote, (partly) bemoaning the death of the political pamphlet

> it might be argued that in England, with its free and reasonably varied press, there is not much scope for the pamphleteer; but this will not be endorsed by anyone who has ever tried to get a bearing for a genuinely unpopular cause. Certainly the British press has juridical freedom, which is not a sham but a very real blessing, and in the modern world an increasingly rare one. But it is not true that the British press adequately represents all shades of opinion. Nearly always it is safe to put one's political opinions on paper, but to get them into print, and still more to get them to a big public, is not so easy. Because of the way in which newspapers are owned and operated, not only can minority opinions – and even majority opinions, when they are not backed by some influential group – go almost unheard, but events of the utmost importance can pass unnoticed or can reach the public only in some shrunken and distorted form. At any given moment there is a sort of all-prevailing orthodoxy, a general tacit agreement not to discuss some large and uncomfortable fact.[292]

Leaving aside questions of accessibility, what about other practicalities, such as guarantees for human safety and liberty in any future society? I will have much more to say about this in part two but, if we were talking about a concrete structure here, it would be possible to build in a safeguard which guaranteed the basic liberties, not only throughout the process

---

[289] See further below.
[290] See pp. 95–96 above.
[291] See the quotation on p. 96 above.
[292] Orwell 1948, p. 16.

itself but also after it. Without such an assurance, it is unlikely that rational human beings would ever agree to enter into the bargaining in the first place,[293] since some of our basic human needs would not be guaranteed. However, since a concrete, referendum-type, structure is, as I have said, unlikely, another possibility is to build those guarantees into the analysis of the different form of socio-political organisation a given author prefers and this is what I shall try to do in part two. Further, of course, human rationality and the logic of decision, if that is of the kind described by Frank Ramsey,[294] will perhaps provide an extra safeguard here – we are unlikely to ascribe to a form of social organisation (if given the actual choice, of course) which does not guarantee our basic needs and, concomitantly, the basic liberties.[295]

What of the democratic structure itself? Is it not likely, if we follow Mill[296] (or Tocqueville), that the democratic mass is likely to prove tyrannical and oppress minorities?

As I have said, a catalogue of basic rights is built into the process to prevent this from happening. No human being, or group of human beings, is immune from the effects of holding power. This said, the age-old dogma regarding the 'tyranny of the majority' is one it is well worth our shedding, just the kind of subjective judgement I have been cautioning against through the present text. This long-held prejudice is based on over two and a half millennia of anti-popular thought,[297] though, in fact, there may be little reason to believe that we, the people, would behave any more tyrannically than our representatives. In fact, in Classical Athens, it was claimed that, far from being oppressive, a participatory democracy allowed its citizens more individual freedom than any other form of political establishment, and the Athenians were criticised for allowing such expansive freedom.[298] It is one

---

[293] That is, going along the lines of Ramsey-style decision theory. See Ramsey 1931.
[294] Ramsey 1931.
[295] Rawls said much the same thing. See Rawls 1996, pp. 315 ff., for example. The difference is that I am not deciding what the rational course of action is – you (together with everyone else) are. I am merely proposing what I think the best, and the most just, outcome.
[296] See Mill 1991, pp. 7 ff.
[297] See Roberts 1994.
[298] For the full story, see Edge 2009 and (Forthcoming A).

of history's great (and largely unacknowledged) ironies that (participatory) democracy's modern opponents chastise it for not allowing its citizens enough freedom, whereas its ancient opponents (who actually lived within it) chastised it for allowing too much.[299]

The Athenian democratic insight is, simply, that, given the choice between more freedom or less from the control of the state, we, the people will go for the former option every time.[300] In other words, power is not wielded by the people, in the participatory democratic account, in order to oppress others and impose a totalitarian regime of tight control and watchfulness upon some or all, but precisely the opposite – to prevent others from doing the same to us. The point, again, is not that the Athenians were right about this, any more than they were wrong. This is just a (highly) subjective theory about politics and individual freedom. Its use for our purposes is that it stands as an interesting counter-claim to the age old 'tyranny of the majority'. It may simply be that, given the choice, we, the people, may actually choose a regime of greater (and more equal – more on which in a moment) individual liberty than that which is imposed upon us by others. That is an interesting thought.

An ultimate problem posed by the questions I began with is that someone has to answer them. No neutral, impartial, solution is waiting for us, just beyond the horizon, as to how we might live together in conditions of freedom and peace and universal justice. A further problem is that these are highly complex problems that require highly complex solutions. But someone, or some group, has to provide an answer. If I am right, and that the solution to the Berlinean problem of positive liberty entails that it should be left to us to find the answers, then yes, we certainly need to build in safeguards to prevent us from wielding power in immoral and amoral ways. But this would hold regardless of whoever was doing the deciding. And yes, no ultimate amount of 'epistemological freedom', to help us undertake this task to the best of our abilities, and as freely as possible, is ever going to be available for everyone. There are too many barriers, too many vested

---

[299] See Edge 2009, pp. 44–45.
[300] See, especially, Edge 2009, pp. 34 ff.

interests, too many vast and intricate complexities of human language and thought, in the way of the final and absolute freedom of the mental. All I think we can do, is try to provide each of us with as much freedom to judge as possible.

Another reason for making this point is to make clear that I am not arguing on behalf of setting up those conditions under which my own conception of justice, my own view as to how political society should be ordered, will be automatically adopted by rational human beings and that, therefore, those who reject it can be forced, since they are after all, rational human beings, to accept it. Not only would this have the clear appearance of a positive liberty doctrine – a perfect illustration of Rousseau's maxim that people might need to be forced to be free [301] – and therefore, as a doctrine, it would have to be automatically rejected, I could personally have no idea what those 'ideal' conditions are.

There are many barriers in the way of free judgement (of the kind I have mentioned and many more besides), but even if they could all be removed, even if a perfect state of epistemological freedom could be attained (which, I would venture to suggest, it cannot), who is to say what our judgement under those conditions would be? My argument, based upon the recognition of first-person authority, is that only we can ultimately provide the answers to these questions. It is also worth repeating that, regardless of whatever we happen to decide, the answer will not be – or is, at least, highly unlikely to be – perfect freedom, or the final, objective, answer to all moral disputes. It is impossible to say whether we, as a species, will ever attain those particular ultimate goals.

The best I think we can do, according to the project I have outlined here, is to put forward the answers, or solutions, we happen to think are best and leave it to others to judge. We are back then, to the fundamental relationship of triangulation, of writer, reader and a shared outside world. Those solutions which are likely to be most successful are those which, very simply, will fare best in these triangular exchanges and I have discussed, in this chapter, ways in which this fundamental triangular relationship can be supported so that our

---

[301] Rousseau 1973,1.7 p. 195.

judgements are freer. This means investigating our language-picture and its accumulated jumble of beliefs and building, from the bottom up, accounts of our normative concepts to challenge the contemporary hegemonic uses we encounter in everyday communication. But it also means approaching the task with genuineness, with open ears and open minds, with an acknowledgement that the right answers are independent of whatever it is we happen to believe. It means a free and open debate conducted according to ideological persuasion and not subjective personal invective, which is something, I suspect, that turns people away from modern politics (and modern political discourse) in large numbers.

You may wish to counter that a belief in our ability to do the right thing – if we *do* now focus on the morally right thing for a moment – is a fairly weak argument for suggesting that we will actually do the right thing were the time, and the opportunity, to come,[302] particularly, perhaps, when there is so much evidence to the contrary. One counter to this is, as Rawls says,

> if a reasonably just Society of Peoples whose members subordinate their power to reasonable aims is not possible, and human beings are largely amoral, if not incurably cynical and self-centred, one might ask, with Kant, whether it is worthwhile for human beings to live on the earth.[303]

However, I think we can go further.

Davidson's argument regarding the objectivity of values[304] not only points to the fundamentally objective nature of value judgements, but also to(wards) our shared ability to judge in an ethical and moral way, to our shared ability, in short, to do the right thing. Furthermore there is a wide range of evidence which actually supports that view – not just the existence and development of moral values in the first place, though human moral development is certainly frustratingly slow, but also the great success, in popular culture and consciousness, of moral

---

[302] As I have been saying throughout, I am also appealing (in part two) to our rational judgement, so far as this differs, or might differ, from our moral judgement. However, in this section, I am just focusing on the latter, our moral judgement.
[303] Rawls 1999b, p. 128.
[304] See above pp. 61–69.

tales in film, fable and fiction (and a number of other forms of media).

Popular moral culture and, the shared values of popular religion, would simply not be what it is if this were not true, at least not in the same way. As Davidson says, "to be able to understand another, I must share her world, in its larger features at least, and this includes its values."[305] So, *The Dark Knight* or, in a much more radical way, Idries Shah's *World Tales*[306] do not work, and could not ever have become successful, not only if we did not share their world, their universe, but also if that same world were not common to all of us. As de Gaynesford said at the end of a review of an interesting recent book about the philosophy of film,[307] "films can indeed philosophize, and in the Heideggerian sense: they can let what shows itself within the world be seen."[308] This is highly significant, and why popular culture often says more about human morality than much academic moral philosophy, though that statement, I am sure, will be no less controversial than those by Ayer and Anscombe I mentioned earlier.

Now, I am not so naive, nor so arrogant, to assume that this means that there is no room for ethical dispute,[309] or that it will be my own answers which will turn out to be ultimately true. The conclusion is far less ambitious and far less dramatic, but still of great significance on its own terms.

Peter Railton has also called for a 'naturalisation' of ethics.[310] I cannot say whether he had in mind anything of the kind I have outlined here, via a stress on first-person authority, to an examination of the linguistic (and epistemological) context within which the contemporary processes of triangulation (the learning of words and concepts and the sharing of ideas through communication) takes place. Nevertheless, it is into these triangular relationships we must place our own answers to the questions I began with. And this is what I have tried to do here and will try to do again, in a much extended way, in part two.

---

[305] See the quotation on p. 62 above and the one below, p. 106.
[306] Shah 1991 – note its subtitle.
[307] Livingston and Plantinga 2008.
[308] De Gaynesford 2009, p. 25.
[309] See pp. 67–68 above.
[310] Railton 1998, p. 251.

Rawls says that the role of political philosophy is to articulate and uncover shared notions in the historical culture of a given society. He says

> the real task is to discover and formulate the deeper bases of agreement which one hopes are embedded in common sense, or even to originate and fashion starting points for common understanding by expressing in a new form the convictions found in the historical tradition by connecting them with a wide range of people's considered convictions.[311]

To an extent, this sums up exactly what I am saying here. I agree that it is the task of political philosophy to investigate our inherited language-picture, and for political philosophers to lay out their own analysis of how (their versions of) alterable human practices will best realise the normative values, freedom, justice, equality and peace chief amongst them, we hold dear. But it seems to me, if I am right, that the agreement will not be formulated by the political philosophy as such, but by how successfully the political philosophy does, in fact, order those concepts. By how well that philosophy, in other words, reflects a shared outside world common to all. As I have argued here, if we are to take the dangers of positive liberty seriously, the judging must not be done by political philosophers, but by each of us as we investigate the various political philosophies and theories which are put before us.

As Davidson says

> we start out assuming that others have, in the basic and largest matters, beliefs and values similar to ours. We are bound to suppose someone we want to understand inhabits our world of macroscopic, more or less enduring, physical objects with familiar causal dispositions; that his world, like ours, contains people with minds and motives; and that he shares with us the desire to find warmth, love, security, and success, and the desire to avoid pain and distress.[312]

Though there are things that complicate these relationships,

---

[311] Rawls 1996, p. 306.
[312] Davidson 2004, p. 183.

particularly around the issue of free judgement, ultimately, the solutions to our political and moral problems, whether looked at rationally or morally, will be those which prove to be most successful in these communicative relationships. They will be those which, when reflecting on and discussing our shared world with another, do, in fact, cause the other to think that those solutions do represent that shared human world the best way possible, the best way (in our sense) of increasing human happiness and reducing human distress. Not only does this require us to refine our interventions into these communicative relationships, and in a number of ways, it also points, with great and enduring hope, to the innate power and ability of those relationships to both see, and do, good. And that is a promising thought indeed.

Conclusion to Part One

Leaving other problems aside for the moment, let me come back, by way of conclusion, to Berlin's definition of simple, negative, liberty. "If I am prevented by others", he writes, "*from doing what I could otherwise do*, I am to that degree unfree."[313] But, just as I argued above with reference to Berlin's attempt to distinguish 'liberty' from 'political liberty', as well as from 'the conditions for its exercise', this will require yet another subjective interpretation, in this case of 'what I could otherwise do'. Under whose terms (and why) are we to consider 'what I could otherwise do'? Who is to consider what are 'alterable human practices', to return to that other elusive phrase of Berlin's, and why? In what ways can we expect and hope those practices to be altered, for what reasons and with what consequences? Clearly these constructions raise far more questions than they answer.

For instance, the political laws of the nation of Great Britain, enacted by the deeds of men and women (mostly men, unfortunately), prevent me from living in a participatory democracy. This is something (other things aside) that I could otherwise do (if things were different, including the coercive laws of my society). On the participatory democratic account, I am prevented from going to the assembly, from speaking in the assembly in front of my fellow citizens, from voting upon laws and other measures and from proposing bills (and other things) to the democratic assembly. These are freedoms that are fundamentally denied to me by the basic structure (including the coercive apparatus) of the society in which I live, by (on one account at least) 'alterable human practices'.

---

[313] Berlin 2002b, p. 169 (my italics).

Conclusion to Part One 109

Further, I am prevented from using Mr Morgan's yacht,[314] from rambling over the fields belonging to a large estate, and from fishing in the local pond owned by an angling club I cannot afford to join. These are among a number of things I could otherwise do if certain other things were different, if for instance, I lived under a system of communal property, not supported by such coercive laws, at least not in the same way. Under these accounts, I would enjoy a much greater amount of negative liberty (whether I chose to make use of that increased freedom or not) than the amount I currently enjoy. In other words, far from being the path to positive liberty tyranny, these different social conditions would give me more freedom (in the simple, Berlinean, negative sense) from the control of others in the first place, or so I would argue.[315]

Of course there is more to it than this. Some aspects of 'what I could otherwise do' are inherently unknowable, as I have already suggested, until we have actually lived through the changed conditions. For instance, if Stephen Holmes were correct, and social productivity and efficiency are better under free-market capitalism than under socialism[316] because of the emotional structure of motivation (or something similar), then perhaps I would not be able to do things under socialism that I could otherwise do under capitalism. For instance, there might be a reduced amount of choice regarding certain objects, certain available paths and opportunities, because social efficiency would not be enough to produce them and would, instead, just meet more basic needs. In other words, the increased efforts that may go into reducing loss of life, reducing homelessness and most of the basic and fundamental forms of human inequality, might result in a reduction of the diversity that has arisen under modern capitalism (particularly as a result of consumerism).[317]

I happen to believe Holmes is quite possibly wrong about this because, among other things, I have an optimistic view of

---

[314] Cf. p. 79 above.
[315] This point is also well made by David Miller in Miller 2006. As I have said, I will take up this argument at much greater length in part two.
[316] See p. 87 above.
[317] This question – together with related matters – is again dealt with in proper depth in part two.

both human nature and of what life (and motivation) would be like under a more egalitarian social structure (and clearly, both of these aspects are tied together). However, I cannot prove this any more than Holmes can. All I can do is put forward as much evidence as I can for my view and leave it for other human beings to judge according to the structure I have outlined here. It is clear that this will be a tough battle to fight. For as many examples of the positive side of human nature as I could cite, my opponent (I am assuming that she exists) will be able to cite counterexamples. And this is just the beginning.

What is needed here, as I suggested in the introduction, is an account of egalitarian equal liberty[318] which counters the adapted version of Rawls' difference principle I mentioned earlier.[319] This means that, among other things, I will have to show how those who are now worse off will do better in terms of individual liberty than they currently do. As I say, I do happen to believe that this is more than possible and not solely in the sense that the realms of individual liberty (actual, genuine, material free choice and opportunity) are more egalitarian, but that these (egalitarian) realms are themselves wider and greater than they are under free-market capitalism, except, perhaps, for those who are, under the current system, very wealthy.

For now, however, I am concerned with liberty and, as I have been emphasising throughout, liberty alone. I wish to conclude this by attempting to pull everything together. Berlin says,

> what troubles the consciences of Western liberals is, I think, the belief, not that the freedom men seek differs according to their social or economic conditions, but that the minority who possess it have gained it by exploiting, or, at least, averting their gaze from, the vast majority who do not. They believe, with good reason, that if individual liberty is an ultimate end for human beings, none should be deprived of it by others; least of all that some should enjoy it at the expense of others. Equality of liberty; not to treat others as I should not wish them to treat me; repayment of my debt to those who alone have made possible

---

[318] I use this phrase to refer to the system I myself put forward in part two.
[319] See pp. 30–31 above.

my liberty or prosperity or enlightenment; justice, in its simplest and most universal sense - these are the foundations of liberal morality."[320]

It is here where I believe that my earlier argument regarding Berlin's arbitrary distinction between 'liberty' and the 'conditions for its exercise' takes on some importance. It is also here that we see, clearly, that what we mean by our contemporary use of the word 'freedom', is so important. If we take it to mean what liberals mean, then an equal amount of basic (Berlinean) 'political freedom' (liberty of conscience, of thought and so on), coupled with raging inequality and its consequences (which Berlin, of course, subsumes under the banner of 'conditions for the exercise of freedom'), is not 'unjust'. However, if a broader understanding of 'liberty' is in linguistic use in that society, then any unequal degrees of liberty in that society can quickly start to look 'unjust' on liberty's terms alone (coupled with equality of course).

Put it this way. Think of some of the major social ills that plague certain human communities around the globe: The cycles of violence that haunt Brazilian *favelas*, where the police even fear to go; millions upon millions living in shanty towns and slums without access to safe, clean, drinking water and other basic needs; millions of human beings living in conflict zones (and all the ills of social oppression and coercion that accompany this, such as human trafficking, child-soldiery, rape, theft and murder) and refugee camps; the thousands who sleep on the streets of Western nations every night because they have nowhere else to go; the men and women forced to risk tiger-infested forests because it is their only way to make a living,[321] and this, as I have been stressing throughout, is barely even scratching the surface of the types and forms of oppression human beings face every day through inequality.

I am simply saying that it is a misuse, and a downgrading, of the term to suggest that these human beings (and many

---

[320] Berlin 2002b, p. 172.
[321] I will discuss these forms of inequality, and provide further references to the literature, in greater detail in part two. An excellent starting point, however, is Pogge 2002 and the essays in Pogge 2007. Sen's example of the tiger-infested Sundarban is also particularly memorable. See Sen 1999, p. 146.

others) possess 'liberty' simply because the issue can be sidestepped by adhering to some subjective theory of coercion, oppression, or doctrine, which separates (so-called) 'political freedom' from 'the conditions for its exercise'.[322] We are talking about liberty and liberty alone. They may, if their society has enacted them according to a system of laws, possess certain 'rights', but if they are deprived of the most basic choices and opportunities, they can hardly be said to be 'free', at least not in any wide sense or degree. Their freedom of choice, their range of genuine, choosable opportunities is so narrow as to be, in many cases, almost obsolete and is, in fact, in many cases, absolutely obsolete.

This is not to say that freedom is synonymous with eating, with having a roof over one's head or with having an education,[323] but rather, that it is a bastardisation of the term to suggest that those whose lives are beset by a lack of genuine, available, choices possess 'liberty' to any wide degree. They may well possess certain forms of liberty (perhaps there is no secret police to investigate their doings, no religious law preventing them expressing themselves sexually as they may wish, no totalising computerised 'thought-searcher' that keeps tabs on their innermost wishes, thoughts and desires) yet, still, their basic area for free movement, in the most simple and basic sense, is heavily restricted. I may not be going to my death on the cross, or at the hands of Athenians handing me hemlock because of the religion I choose to practice, but if I am a seven year old Kenyan boy dying of starvation the small amount of liberty I might possess, as important as it might be (which I in no way mean to deny[324]), can still not

---

[322] Cf. Edge (Forthcoming B) on what lies beneath the 'surface of meaning'. Cf. pp. 73–74 above.

[323] Though such conditions or choices might be fundamental to human freedom, as is in fact the case with these three, as I have discussed in the main text.

[324] I wish to stress this point. In no way am I saying that these freedoms are valueless or unimportant. Berlin is correct to point out that reformers, in their zeal for economic reforms on behalf of equality, might be prone to forget the value of certain basic liberties (of conscience, of thought, of sexuality and so on). My point is, rather, that the meaning of 'basic liberties' here needs to be extended far wider otherwise vital freedoms can be forgotten – just as Berlin claimed when arguing for (what I have termed) the 'arbitrary distinction'. See Berlin 2002a, p. 46 and pp. 18 ff above.

preserve my life, the life upon which all my future liberty and pursuit of happiness must be based. One of the most simple and basic choices necessary to human freedom, the choice to eat or to refrain from eating, is denied to me.

Berlin says:

> useless freedoms should be made usable, but they are not identical with the conditions indispensable for their utility. This is not a merely pedantic distinction, for if it is ignored, the meaning and value of freedom of choice is apt to be downgraded. In their zeal to create social and economic conditions in which alone freedom is of genuine value, men tend to forget freedom itself; and if it is remembered, it is liable to be pushed aside to make room for these other values with which the reformers or revolutionaries have become preoccupied.[325]

But equally, we must recognise that the point works the other way around. By confusing liberty with some subjective theory of political, economic or social freedom,[326] liberty itself, the idea of genuine and available material choice and opportunity is in danger of being forgotten, and as I have just been arguing, "freedom of choice is apt to be downgraded."

In other words, I am simply urging his own point against Berlin. In their (fully humanistic, sincere and well-intentioned, we need not doubt[327]) attempts to endorse and to secure conditions in which (Berlin's version of) 'political freedom' (liberty of speech, liberty of conscience, liberty of association, liberty of sexual expression and so on) is genuinely enshrined, equally and for all, in political and constitutional life (through a catalogue of basic rights, the rule of law and other constitutional guarantees), liberals may have forgotten the value of freedom itself, the value of actual and genuine available choice and opportunity, and downgraded the importance of material free choice. As I said earlier, freedom of choice and opportunity, the 'doing of my own good in my own way', does not stop being valuable to human beings when the constraint, coercion, or prohibition, is non-human, even if it is non-human. Further, if we added the word 'deliberate' to this situation, as Berlin does, the matter

---

[325] Berlin 2002a, p. 46.
[326] As Berlin does. See my discussion above, pp. 20 ff.
[327] See p. 20 above.

becomes more complex, and more controversial still.

It is not that we should forget liberty of conscience, speech or association, liberty of sexual choice (or any other basic freedom) when constructing our social and political worlds, but the opposite. We must not displace other liberties and freedoms which are absolutely fundamental to freedom of choice and opportunity but, instead, expand the realm of simple, negative, freedom (an area free from coercion, oppression, restraint or constraint, of whatever form that may happen to take) to include all of these. By focusing solely on (what are commonly known as) the 'basic liberties',[328] other freedoms fundamental to human liberty are likely to be forgotten and/or displaced.

Without the arbitrary distinction equality of liberty means an equal access to the choices and opportunities that are available to all within society, not only those freedoms that are basic to liberal analyses. Not that everyone will want to make use of the same choices or opportunities in the same way, nor that they will be able to.[329] This is the beauty of human diversity and it also points to the fact that, if each of us *is* given an equal opportunity to develop those natural talents and abilities we each possess and enjoy differently from one another, then society (and we can suspect, social freedom) will greatly benefit.

It is clear that this is a radical commitment and it is here that we can understand why liberals (and many others) do want to sign up to Berlin's distinction. If equality of individual liberty means only equality of basic rights (freedom of speech, conscience, thought and so on), and if a truly 'unacceptable', or 'unjust', loss of freedom is brought about only according to some arguably pretty spurious theory of intentional human coercion, then no radical commitment to egalitarian conditions follows, since this, in many parts of the West and beyond, is the world we inhabit. If, however, it is taken to mean what it implies, i.e., equality of individual liberty period, this then entails a moral commitment to a very different form of social ordering (similar in basic structure at least, to the one I have outlined very briefly above and will detail in part two) from

---

[328] Cf. Rawls 1996, Lecture 8, pp. 288–371.
[329] As discussed in the example on pp. 79–80 above.

the one we currently inhabit, since it is clear that the amount of (simple, negative) liberty humans possess differs very markedly from one to the next.

The freedom we enjoy (or, as is frequently the case, don't enjoy) is vastly unequal and with catastrophic consequences in many cases. Equality of individual liberty, or, as I call it, egalitarian equal liberty, implies a radical social and political world, a world where, in short, opportunities and choices become communalised, and become available to all, according to what each of us is as an individual human being, where inequalities in freedom, beyond those based on (fully developed) individual abilities, are unacceptable and unjust. More is needed to show that such a world can be sustainable, peaceful and successful and can meet the kind of Rawlsian criteria I have discussed, and I do not shy away from that, but even if the attempt fails, this does not ultimately diminish the demands of justice. And furthermore, this is not a form of justice I have invented, the words are Berlin's – "Equality of liberty; not to treat others as I should not wish them to treat me … justice, in its simplest and most universal sense."[330]

However, as I have been arguing throughout, liberals have a way out of this. To quote Berlin again on the same theme.

> Nothing is gained by a *confusion* of terms. To avoid glaring inequality or widespread misery I am ready to sacrifice some, or all, of my freedom … But a sacrifice is not an increase in what is being sacrificed, namely freedom…Everything is what it is: liberty is liberty, not equality or fairness or justice or culture, or human happiness or a quiet conscience.[331]

H.L.A. Hart agrees, saying,

> freedom (the absence of coercion) can be *valueless* to those victims of unrestricted competition too poor to make use of it; so it will be pedantic to point out to them that though starving they are free. This is the truth exaggerated by Marxists, whose *identification* of poverty with lack of freedom *confuses* too different evils.[332]

---
[330] I quoted this passage in full, p. 110 above.
[331] Berlin 2002b, p. 172 (my italics).
[332] Hart 1984, n. 2 p. 77 (my italics). This is another excellent example of the kind of linguistic battle I have been discussing throughout. The kind of

I doubt that the confusion belongs to the "Marxists" and, further, this is a claim that goes back to a time well before Marx. Plutarch, in fact, preserved it in his description of the ideological milieu in ancient Syracuse, following its liberation from Dionysius II in the mid-fourth century BC. Plutarch reports the view of the Syracusan demagogue Herakleides as being, "equality was the basis of freedom, whilst slavery was based on the poverty of those without possessions."[333] My argument is that it is not a "confusion" of two different evils, but rather, that the poor, as this Herakleidan view suggests, lack "liberty" and liberty period, because on this analysis, they lack genuine choice, opportunity and possibility in their lives, freedoms and opportunities which are being enjoyed by others.

There is clearly a sense in which Berlin and Hart are correct. 'Equal liberty' does not mean (or equate to) 'liberty' period. It means (if it is not too obvious to say) an equal amount of (whatever we mean by) liberty. Therefore, in turn, what we mean by liberty becomes absolutely key and it is here where theories of coercion and restraint begin to intrude when they do not yet belong.

It is worth remembering here the argument of another liberal, Bernard Williams. When anyone, Williams powerfully argued, makes a claim that they have suffered a loss of freedom, we should take them at face value and consider what should be done about it, for the consequences could be horrifying if we do not.[334] Perhaps, I would add, similar to those Berlin identified throughout his discussion of positive freedom. So for example, when Nelson Mandela, again no Marxist, says,

> like slavery and apartheid, poverty is not natural. It is man-made and it can be overcome and eradicated by the actions of human beings. And overcoming poverty is not a gesture of charity. It is an act of justice. It is the protection of a fundamental human

---

analysis I am advocating helps us to see that these so-called "confusions" are, in fact, no such thing.

[333] Plutarch, *Dion* 37. 3. See Fuks 1984, pp. 213–229 for a full discussion.
[334] Williams 2005a, esp. p. 85.

Conclusion to Part One

right. While poverty persists, there is no true freedom.[335]

I think that we should take him at face value.

As I say, the consequences of not doing so might begin to approach those I have been concerned with, following Berlin, throughout this essay. For as we have seen, the response has tended not to be mere disagreement with Mandela and those who think like him, such as myself, but deeper, that we are guilty of 'philosophical mistakes', 'errors' and 'confusions', that, simply, we are wrong. Though, as I have been urging throughout, the consequences of not adhering to Williams' simple plea and taking those who speak of unfreedom at face value, are that we might allow fragrantly immoral and unjust conditions, of unequal freedom, to endure, because of some spurious and subjective theory of a related, but not identical concept, such as coercion.

This is not to say that disagreements will not, and should not, exist. To the absolute contrary and, as the great treatises for freedom of speech have all argued, from Milton's *Areopagitica* to Berlin's 'Two Concepts of Liberty' and beyond, freedom itself has tended to flourish where vehement disagreement and argument have flourished. But these should be disagreements of another kind, not about freedom and the so-called 'conditions for its exercise' and so on. Instead, I would argue, these should be disagreements about how different sets of alterable human practices do, in fact, constrain and liberate human beings and what can be done about those practices to improve human flourishing. In part two, as I have said, I will put forward my own view on this, but it is to others, liberals, anarchists, conservatives, those who believe in a different form of socialism from mine and many more besides, to disagree. Yes, these arguments will inevitably involve disputes about things like the relationship of the common market and human labour to diversity and resources, efficiency, psychology, human nature, co-operation and the sustainability of different forms of social relations. And freedom itself will be no more identifiable with my view, or anyone else's, than it will be with liberalism. We must detach these disputes from the concept of freedom since, if

---
[335] Mandela 2005.

we don't, we are in danger of forgetting freedom itself and all of the ways in which it can be forgotten, downtrodden and destroyed. The dispute then becomes not about freedom itself, but about how our alterable human practices can be adjusted to prevent human freedom from being negated and annihilated, even when those negations are not the result of direct human behaviour.

These are complex disputes and debates, but it certainly does not help to answer the problem by ducking the issues, by adhering to subjective accounts and theories which might, after all, forget the basic value (freedom, in this case) under consideration. To ignore, or dismiss, individual claims to losses of freedom as "confused" or "mistaken" is to forget, or minimise, the ways in which freedom actually is constrained and thereby, to ignore the much larger question of how we can adapt our societies to prevent those kinds of constraints happening in the future. We may not be able to do something about it in all cases – this is what much of the coming argument will be about – but it will still not help to duck, or ignore, the issue in the first place.

If we are to take the problem of positive liberty at all seriously (and, remember again, that this problem emerged from a liberal analysis in the first place), this requires an acknowledgement of first-person authority which, or so I have argued, means leaving the answering of the fundamental questions of political philosophy to each of us, and not prejudging the outcome according to some subjective theory, assumption, or prejudice regarding human rationality, the natural makeup of political society, the innocent play of social forces or, as I have just been stressing, some supposedly neutral take on the meaning of 'liberty', expressed through contemporary language (among a possible multitude of similar views and claims). This task also requires us to have the opportunity, as well as the platform, to undertake it openly and freely. To pre-empt the outcome would be to defeat the entire process.

It may be our solution and our choice (and this applies whatever the solution or choice may happen to be), but it does not follow that it will be the solution for those who follow us. We must also give them the best opportunity possible for

Conclusion to Part One

ordering their world in the way they wish, and this implies a lasting commitment to the kind of project I have tried to outline in this chapter.[336] This means simply that language, meaning and the acquisition of knowledge are fundamental to political philosophy and equally, that political philosophy is fundamental to each and every one of us. If this condition obtains, political philosophy will perhaps be fulfilling the role that Wittgenstein posited for philosophy in general.[337] By preventing bewitchment we greatly assist the process by which judgement becomes free and this is the point where any analysis of liberty must begin and, ironically, where it must also end.

---

[336] Or, as Tom Paine famously put it, "if the present generation, or any other, are disposed to be slaves, it does not lessen the right of the succeeding generation to be free." Paine 1984, p. 124.
[337] See p. 53 above.

Bibliography

Anscombe, G.E.M. (1997). 'Modern Moral Philosophy' in R. Crisp and M. Slote (eds.), *Virtue Ethics* (Oxford), pp. 26–44. [Originally 1958]

Austin, J.L. (1962). *How to do Things with Words* (Oxford. Ed. J.O. Urmson).

Ayer, A.J. (2001). *Language, Truth and Logic* (New repr. London). [Originally 1936]

Bales, Kevin (1999). *Disposable People: New Slavery in the Global Economy* (Berkeley).

Barber, Benjamin (1984). *Strong Democracy: Participatory Politics for a New Age* (Berkeley).

Berlin, Isaiah (2002a). 'Introduction' to *Liberty* (Oxford. Ed. H. Hardy), pp. 3–54. [Originally 1969]

Berlin, Isaiah (2002b). 'Two Concepts of Liberty' in Berlin, *Liberty* (Oxford. Ed. H. Hardy), pp. 166–217. [Originally 1958]

Berlin, Isaiah (2002c). 'From Hope and Fear Set Free' in Berlin, *Liberty* (Oxford. Ed. H. Hardy), pp.252–279. [Originally 1964]

Berlin, Isaiah (2002d). *Freedom and its Betrayal: Six Enemies of Human Liberty* (London. Ed. H. Hardy). [Originally 1952]

Berlin, Isaiah (2002e). 'Liberty' in Berlin, *Liberty* (Oxford. Ed. H. Hardy), pp. 283–286. [Originally 1995]

Blackburn, Simon (1985). 'Error and the Phenomenology of Value' in T. Honderich (ed.), *Morality and Objectivity: A Tribute to J.L. Mackie* (London), pp. 1–22.

Brown, G. (2007). 'Speech on Liberty' (25th October 2007). Available at http://www.number10.gov.uk/Page13630 [Accessed 25th September 2009].

Carter, Ian (1999). *A Measure of Freedom* (Oxford).

Carter, Ian (2008). 'How are Power and Freedom Related?' in C. Laborde and J. Maynor (eds.), *Republicanism and Political Theory* (Malden), pp. 58–82.

Cartledge, Paul (2009). *Ancient Greek Political Thought in Practice* (Cambridge).

Cartledge, Paul and Edge, Matt (2009). '"Rights", Individuals and Communities in Ancient Greece' in R. Balot (ed.), *A Companion to Greek and Roman Political Thought* (Oxford), Chapter 10.

Cohen, G.A. (1979). 'Capitalism, Freedom and the Proletariat' in A. Ryan (ed.), *The Idea of Freedom: Essays in Honour of Isaiah Berlin* (Oxford), pp. 9–25.

Constant, Benjamin (1988a). 'The Spirit of Conquest and Usurpation and their Relation to European Civilisation' in *Constant: Political Writings* (Cambridge. Ed. B. Fontana), pp. 44–167. [Originally 1814]

Constant, Benjamin (1988b). 'The Liberty of the Ancients Compared with that of the Moderns' in *Constant: Political Writings* (Cambridge. Ed. B. Fontana), pp. 309–328. [Originally 1819]

Constant, Benjamin (1988c). 'Principles of Politics Applicable to All Representative Governments' in Constant, *Political Writings* (Cambridge. Ed. B. Fontana), pp. 169–305. [Originally 1815]

Davidson, Donald (2001a). *Inquiries into Truth and Interpretation* (New ed., Oxford).

Davidson, Donald (2001b). *Subjective, Intersubjective, Objective* (Oxford).

Davidson, Donald (2001c). 'Psychology as Philosophy' in Davidson, *Essays on Actions and Events* (2nd ed. Oxford), pp. 229–244. [Originally 1974]

Davidson, Donald (2001d). 'How is Weakness of the Will Possible?' in Davidson, *Essays on Actions and Events* (2nd ed., Oxford), pp. 21–24. [Originally 1969]

Davidson, Donald (2004). *Problems of Rationality* (Oxford).

Davidson, Donald (2005). *Truth, Language and History* (Oxford).

De Gaynesford, Maximilian (2009). 'Heart of the Heart of the Matter' (Review of Livingston and Plantinga 2008), *TLS October 2nd 2009*, pp. 24–25.

Dunn, John (1990). 'Liberty as a Substantive Political Value' in J. Dunn, *Interpreting Political Responsibility: Essays 1981–1989* (Cambridge), pp. 61–84. [Originally 1984]

Dunn, John (1993). *Western Political Theory in the Face of the Future* (New ed., Cambridge).

Dworkin, Ronald (1978). 'Liberalism' in S. Hampshire (ed.), *Public and Private Morality* (Cambridge), pp. 113–143.

Dworkin, Ronald (1981). 'What is Equality? Part 2: Equality of Resources', *Philosophy and Public Affairs*, 10 (4), pp. 283–345. Repr. in Dworkin 2000, pp. 65–119.

Dworkin, Ronald (1991). 'Two Concepts of Liberty' in E. Margalit and A. Margalit (eds.), *Isaiah Berlin: A Celebration* (London), pp. 100–109.

Dworkin, Ronald (2000). *Sovereign Virtue: The Theory and Practice of Equality* (Harvard).
Edge, Matt (2009). 'Athens and the Spectrum of Liberty', *History of Political Thought*, 30 (1), pp. 1–45.
Edge, Matt (Forthcoming A). 'Two Concepts of Democracy'.
Edge, Matt (Forthcoming B). 'The Spectrum of Liberty'.
Edge, Matt (Forthcoming C). *On Liberty and Peace, Part Two: Peace* (Exeter, 2011).
Edge, Matt (Forthcoming D). 'Liberty, Authenticity and the Freedom of the Will'.
Einstein, Albert (1942). 'Freedom and Science' in R.N. Anshen (ed.), *Freedom: Its Meaning* (London), pp. 91–93.
Elliot, J. (ed.) (1861). *The Debates in the Several State Conventions on the Adoption of the Federal Constitution as Recommended by the General Convention at Philadelphia* (Philadelphia).
Fontana, Biancamaria (1988). 'Introduction' to *Constant: Political Writings* (Cambridge. Ed. Fontana), pp. 1–42.
Frege, Gottlob (1977). *Logical Investigations* (Oxford. Ed. P.T. Geach). [Originally 1918–1923]
Fuks, Alexander (1984). *Social Conflict in Ancient Greece* (Jerusalem).
Gandhi, M.K. (1997). *Hind Swaraj* in Gandhi, *Hind Swaraj and Other Writings* (Cambridge. Ed. A.J. Parel), pp. 1–125. [Originally 1909]
Geuss, Raymond (1995). 'Freedom as an Ideal', *The Aristotelian Society: Supplementary Volume*, 69, pp. 87–100.
Goody, Jack (2007). *The Theft of History* (Cambridge).
Gray, John N. (1980). 'On Negative and Positive Liberty', *Political Studies*, 28, pp. 507–526.
Grice, H.P. (1957). 'Meaning', *The Philosophical Review*, 66, pp. 377–387.
Grice, H.P. (1969). 'Utterer's Meaning and Intentions', *The Philosophical Review*, 78, pp. 147–177.
Habermas, J. (1996). *Between Facts and Norms* (Cambridge. Trans. W. Rehg). [Originally 1992]
Habermas, J. (1997). 'Kant's Idea of Perpetual Peace, with the Benefit of Two Hundred Years' Hindsight' in J. Bohman and M. Lutz-Bachmann (eds.), *Perpetual Peace: Essays on Kant's Cosmopolitan Ideal* (Cambridge, Mass.), pp. 113–153.
Hamilton, Alexander, Madison, James and Jay, John (2003). *The Federalist* (Cambridge. Ed. T. Ball). [Originally 1788]
Harris, Ian (2002). 'Berlin and his Critics' in I. Berlin, *Liberty* (Oxford. Ed. H. Hardy), pp. 349–366.
Hart, H.L.A. (1984). 'Are there Any Natural Rights?' in J. Waldron (ed.), *Theories of Rights* (Oxford), pp. 77–96. [Originally 1955]

Harvey, F.D. (1965). 'Two Kinds of Equality', *Classica et Mediaevalia*, 26, pp. 101–146.

Heidegger, Martin (1993). 'The Self-Assertion of the German University' in R. Wolin (ed.), *The Heidegger Controversy* (Cambridge, Mass.), pp. 29–39. [Originally 1933]

Heidegger, Martin (2002). *The Essence of Truth* (London. Trans. T. Sadler). [Originally 1932]

Hirschmann, Nancy J. (2002). *The Subject of Liberty: Toward a Feminist Theory of Freedom* (Princeton).

Holmes, Stephen (1984). *Benjamin Constant and the Making of Modern Liberalism* (New Haven).

Holmes, Stephen (1989). 'The Permanent Structure of Antiliberal Thought' in N.L. Rosenblum (ed.), *Liberalism and the Moral Life* (Cambridge, Mass.), pp. 227–253.

Holmes, Stephen (1995). *Passions and Constraint: On the Theory of Liberal Democracy* (Chicago).

Howland, D. (2001). 'Translating Liberty in Nineteenth-Century Japan', *Journal of the History of Ideas*, 62, pp. 161–181.

Hume, David (1997). *An Enquiry Concerning the Principles of Morals* (Oxford, ed. T.L. Beauchamp). [Originally 1751]

Kant, Immanuel (1996). 'Toward Perpetual Peace: A Philosophical Sketch' in Kant, *Practical Philosophy* (Cambridge. Ed. M.J. Gregor), pp. 311–351. [Originally1795]

Kramer, Matthew H. (2003). *The Quality of Freedom* (Oxford).

Kramer, Matthew H. (2008). 'Liberty and Domination' in C. Laborde and J. Maynor (eds.), *Republicanism and Political Theory* (Malden), pp. 31–57.

Kropotkin, Peter (1995). *The Conquest of Bread* in Kropotkin, *The Conquest of Bread and Other Anarchist Writings* (Cambridge. Ed. M.S. Shatz), pp. 1–199. [English ed., Originally 1913]

Livingston, Paisley and Plantinga, Carl (eds.) (2008). *The Routledge Companion to Philosophy and Film* (London).

Lukes, Steven (1973). 'On the Social Determination of Truth' in R. Horton and R. Finnegan (eds.), *Modes of Thought* (London), pp. 230–248.

MacCallum, Gerald C. (1967). 'Negative and Positive Freedom', *Philosophical Review*, 76, pp. 312–334.

Mackie, J.L. (1977). *Ethics: Inventing Right and Wrong* (London).

Maclean, P.D. (1980). 'Sensory and Perceptive Factors in Emotional Functions of the Triune Brain' in A.O. Rorty (ed.), *Explaining Emotions* (Berkeley), pp. 9–36. [Originally 1975]

Mandela, Nelson (2005). 'Speech of 3rd February 2005' available at http://news.bbc.co.uk/1/hi/uk_politics/4232603.stm [Accessed 01/October/2009]

Manin, Bernard (1997). *The Principles of Representative Government* (Cambridge).
Martin, B. (1999). 'Interpretation and Responsibility: Excavating Davidson's Ethical Theory' in L.E. Hahn (ed.), *The Philosophy of Donald Davidson* (Chicago), pp. 345–356.
Marx, Karl (1934). *The Class Struggles in France* (London. Ed. C.P. Dutt). [Originally 1850]
Marx, Karl (1936a). *The Poverty of Philosophy* (London. Eds. C.P. Dutt and V. Chattopadhyaya). [Originally 1846–1847]
Marx, Karl (1936b). 'Address on the Question of Free Trade' in Marx, *The Poverty of Philosophy* (London. Eds. C.P. Dutt and V. Chattopadhyaya), pp. 194–208. [Originally 1848]
Marx, Karl (1975a). 'On the Jewish Question' in Marx, *Early Writings* (London. Trans. G. Benton), pp. 211–241. [Originally 1843]
Marx, Karl (1975b). 'A Contribution to the Critique of Hegel's Philosophy of Right: Introduction' in Marx, *Early Writings* (London, 1975. Trans. G. Benton), pp. 243–257. [Originally 1843–1844]
Marx, Karl (1975c). 'The Economic and Philosophical Manuscripts' in Marx, *Early Writings* (London. Trans. G. Benton), pp. 280–400. [Originally 1844]
Marx, Karl (1975d). 'Letter to Ruge, Cologne, May 1843' in Marx, *Early Writings* (London. Trans. G. Benton), pp. 200–206. [Originally 1843]
Marx, Karl (1996a). 'The Eighteenth Brumaire of Louis Bonaparte' in Marx, *Later Political Writings* (Cambridge. Ed. T. Carver), pp. 31–127. [Originally 1851–1852]
Marx, Karl (1996b). 'The Civil War in France' in Marx, *Later Political Writings* (Cambridge. Ed. T. Carver), pp. 163–207. [Originally 1871]
Marx, Karl (1996c). 'Critique of the Gotha Programme' in Marx, *Later Political Writings* (Cambridge. Ed. T. Carver), pp. 208–226. [Originally 1875]
Marx, Karl and Engels, Friedrich (1974). *The German Ideology* (London. Ed. C.J. Arthur). [Originally 1845–1846]
Marx, Karl and Engels, Friedrich (1992). *The Communist Manifesto* (Oxford. Trans. D. McLellan). [Originally 1848]
McCloskey, H.J. (1965). 'A Critique of the Ideals of Liberty', *Mind*, 74, pp. 483–508.
McDowell, J. (1976). 'Truth Conditions, Bivalence and Verificationism' in G. Evans and J. McDowell (eds.), *Truth and Meaning* (Oxford), pp. 42–66.
Megone, C. (1987). 'One Concept of Liberty', *Political Studies*, 35, pp. 611–622.

Metz, Thaddeus (2007). 'Towards an African Moral Theory', *Journal of Political Philosophy*, 15 (3), pp. 321–341.
Mill, John Stuart (1991). 'On Liberty' in Mill, *On Liberty and Other Essays* (Oxford. Ed. J. Gray), pp. 5–128. [Originally 1859]
Miller, David (2006). 'Introduction' to Miller, *The Liberty Reader* (2nd rev. ed., Edinburgh), pp. 1–20.
Nelson, Eric (2004). *The Greek Tradition in Republican Thought* (Cambridge).
Nelson, Eric (2005). 'Liberty: One Concept Too Many?', *Political Theory*, 33, pp. 58–78.
Nicholls, D. (1962). 'Positive Liberty, 1880–1914', *American Political Science Review*, 56, pp. 114–128.
Orwell, George (1948). 'Introduction' to G. Orwell and R. Reynolds (eds.), *British Pamphleteers* (London), pp. 7–16.
Oswald, John (1995). 'The Government of the People' in G. Claeys (ed.), *Political Writings of the 1790's, volume 4: Radicalism and Reform 1793–1800* (London), pp. 95–103. [Originally 1793]
Paine, Thomas (1984). *The Rights of Man* (New York. Ed. E. Foner). [Originally 1791]
Palmer, R.R. (1953). 'Notes on the Use of the Word "Democracy" 1789–1799', *Political Science Quarterly*, 68, pp. 203–226.
Pettit, Philip (1993). 'Negative Liberty, Liberal and Republican', *European Journal of Philosophy*, 1, pp. 15–38.
Pettit, Philip (1997). *Republicanism: A Theory of Freedom and Government* (Oxford).
Pettit, Philip (1999). 'Republican Freedom and Contestatory Democratisation' in I. Shapiro and C. Hacker-Cordón (eds.), *Democracy's Value* (Cambridge), pp. 163–190.
Pettit, Philip (2007). 'Free Persons and Free Choices', *History of Political Thought*, 28 (4), pp. 709–718.
Pettit, Philip (2008). 'Republican Freedom: Three Axioms, Four Theorems' in C. Laborde and J. Maynor (eds.), *Republicanism and Political Theory* (Malden), pp. 102–130.
Pitkin, Hanna F. (1967). *The Concept of Representation* (Berkeley).
Pitkin, Hanna F. (1989). 'Representation' in T. Ball, J. Farr and R.L. Hanson (eds.), *Political Innovation and Conceptual Change* (Cambridge), pp. 132–154.
Plotke, David (1997). 'Representation is Democracy', *Constellations*, 4, pp. 19–34.
Pocock, J.G.A. (1975). *The Machiavellian Moment: Florentine Political Thought and the Atlantic Republican Tradition* (Princeton).
Pocock, J.G.A. (1985a). 'Introduction: The State of the Art' in Pocock, *Virtue, Commerce and History* (Cambridge), pp. 1–34.

Pocock, J.G.A. (1985b). 'Virtues, Rights and Manners: A Model for Historians of Political Thought' in Pocock, *Virtue, Commerce and History* (Cambridge), pp. 37–50. [Originally 1981]

Pocock, J.G.A. (1989). 'Languages and their Implications: The Transformation of the Study of Political Thought' in Pocock, *Politics, Language and Time* (Chicago), pp. 3–41. [Originally 1971]

Pogge, Thomas (2002). *World Poverty and Human Rights* (Oxford).

Pogge, Thomas (2007) (ed.). *Freedom from Poverty as a Human Right* (Oxford).

Putnam, Hilary (1975a). 'The Meaning of "Meaning"' in Putnam, *Mind, Language And Reality: Philosophical Papers, volume 2* (Cambridge), pp. 215–271. [Originally 1975]

Putnam, Hilary (1975b). 'Language and Reality' in Putnam, *Mind, Language and Reality: Philosophical Papers, volume 2* (Cambridge), pp. 272–290. [Originally 1974]

Putnam, Hilary (2002). *The Collapse of the Fact/Value Dichotomy and Other Essays* (Cambridge, Mass.).

Quine, W.V. (1969a). 'Epistemology Naturalised' in Quine, *Ontological Relativity and Other Essays* (New York), pp. 69–90. [Originally 1965]

Quine, W.V. (1969b). 'Ontological Relativity' in Quine, *Ontological Relativity and Other Essays* (New York), pp. 26–68. [Originally 1968]

Quine, W.V. (1977). 'Facts of the Matter' in R.W. Shahan and K.R. Merrill (eds.), *American Philosophy from Edwards to Quine* (Norman), pp. 176–196.

Quine, W.V. (1980a). 'On What there is' in Quine, *From a Logical Point of View* (2nd rev. ed., Cambridge, Mass.), pp. 1–19. [Originally 1948]

Quine, W.V. (1980b). 'Two Dogmas of Empiricism' in Quine, *From a Logical Point Of View* (2nd rev. ed., Cambridge, Mass.), pp. 20–46. [Originally 1951]

Quine, W.V. (1980c). 'The Problem of Meaning in Linguistics' in Quine, *From a Logical Point of View* (2nd rev. ed., Cambridge, Mass.), pp. 47–64. [Originally 1951]

Quine, W.V. (1981a). 'On the Very Idea of a Third Dogma' in Quine, *Theories and Things* (Harvard), pp. 38–42.

Quine, W.V. (1981b) 'Things and their Place in Theories' in Quine, *Theories and Things* (Cambridge, Mass.), pp. 1–23.

Quine, W.V. (1981c). 'On the Nature of Moral Values' in Quine, *Theories and Things* (Cambridge, Mass.), pp. 55–66. [Originally 1978]

Quine, W.V. (1992). *Pursuit of Truth* (Rev. ed, Cambridge, Mass., 1992).

Bibliography

Quine, W.V. (1999). 'Where do we Disagree?' in L.E. Hahn (ed.), *The Philosophy of Donald Davidson* (Chicago), pp. 73–79.

Railton, Peter (1998). 'Alienation, Consequentialism, and the Demands of Morality' in J. Rachels (ed.), *Ethical Theory 2: Theories about How We Should Live* (Oxford), pp. 222–255 [Originally 1984]

Ramsey, Frank P. (1931). 'Truth and Probability' in Ramsey, *Foundations of Mathematics* (London. Ed. R.B. Braithwaite), pp. 156–198. [Originally 1926]

Raphael, D.D. (1983). 'Liberty and Authority' in A. Phillips Griffiths (ed.), *Of Liberty* (Cambridge), pp. 1–15.

Rawls, John (1982). 'Social Utility and Primary Goods' in A. Sen and B. Williams (eds.), *Utilitarianism and Beyond* (Cambridge), pp. 159–185.

Rawls, John (1996). *Political Liberalism* (Rev. ed., New York).

Rawls, John (1998). 'Justice as Fairness' in J. Rachels (ed.), *Ethical Theory 2: Theories about How We Should Live* (Oxford), pp. 76–101. [Originally 1958]

Rawls, John (1999a). *A Theory of Justice* (Rev. ed., Oxford).

Rawls, John (1999b). *The Law of Peoples* (Harvard).

Rawls, John (1999c). 'Justice as Fairness: Political not Metaphysical' in Rawls, *Collected Papers* (Cambridge, Mass.), pp. 388–414. [Originally 1985]

Rawls, John (1999d). 'Kantian Constructivism in Moral Theory' Rawls, *Collected Papers* (Cambridge, Mass.), pp. 303–358. [Originally 1980]

Rawls, John (2001). *Justice as Fairness: A Restatement* (Cambridge, Mass. Ed. E. Kelly).

Raz, Joseph (1986). *The Morality of Freedom* (Oxford).

Roberts, J.T. (1994). *Athens on Trial: The Antidemocratic Tradition in Western Thought* (Princeton).

Rorty, Richard (1991). 'The Priority of Democracy to Philosophy ' in Rorty, *Objectivity, Relativism and Truth: Philosophical Papers, volume 1* (Cambridge), pp. 175–196. [Originally 1984]

Rorty, Richard (2005). 'Review of Davidson, *Problems of Rationality*' available at http://ndpr.nd.edu/review.cfm?id=1681 (accessed 01/10/2009).

Rousseau, Jean-Jacques (1973). *The Social Contract* in Rousseau, *The Social Contract and Discourses* (London. Trans. G.D.H. Cole), pp. 180–309. [Originally 1762]

Ryle, Gilbert (1990a). 'Thinking and Language' in Ryle, *Collected Papers, volume 2* (Bristol), pp. 258–271. [Originally 1951]

Ryle, Gilbert (1990b). 'Ordinary Language' in Ryle, *Collected Papers, volume 2* (Bristol), pp. 301–318. [Originally 1953]

Schochet, G.J. (1993). 'Why Should History Matter? Political Theory and the History of Discourse' in J.G.A. Pocock, G.J. Schochet and R.G. Schwoerer (eds.), *The Varieties of British Political Thought, 1500–1800* (Cambridge), pp. 321–357.
Sellars, Wilfrid (1974). 'Conceptual Change' in Sellars, *Essays in Philosophy and its History* (Dordrecht), pp. 172–188. [Originally 1973]
Sen, Amartya (1999). *Development as Freedom* (Oxford).
Shah, Idries (1991). *World Tales: The Extraordinary Coincidence of Stories Told in All Times, in All Places* (London).
Skinner, Quentin (1978). *The Foundations of Modern Political Thought, volume 1: The Renaissance* (Cambridge).
Skinner, Quentin (1984). 'The Idea of Negative Liberty: Philosophical and Historical Perspectives' in R. Rorty, J.B. Schneewind and Q. Skinner (eds.), *Philosophy in History* (Cambridge), pp. 193–221.
Skinner, Quentin (1986). 'The Paradoxes of Political Liberty' in S.M. McMurrin (ed.), *The Tanner Lectures on Human Values VII* (Salt Lake City), pp. 225–250.
Skinner, Quentin (1992a). 'On Justice, the Common Good and the Priority of Liberty' in C. Mouffe (ed.), *Dimensions of Radical Democracy* (London), pp. 211–224.
Skinner, Quentin (1992b). 'The Italian City-Republics' in J. Dunn (ed.), *Democracy: The Unfinished Journey, 508 B.C.–A.D. 1993* (Oxford), pp. 57–69.
Skinner, Quentin (1998). *Liberty Before Liberalism* (Cambridge).
Skinner, Quentin (2001). 'A Third Concept of Liberty', *Proceedings of the British Academy*, 119 (2001 lectures), pp. 237–268.
Skinner, Quentin (2002a). *Visions of Politics, volume 1* (Cambridge).
Skinner, Quentin (2002b). 'Machiavelli on *Virtù* and the Maintenance of Liberty' in Skinner, *Visions of Politics, volume 2* (Cambridge), pp. 160–185. [Originally 1990]
Skinner, Quentin (2002c). 'The Rediscovery of Republican Values' in Skinner, *Visions of Politics, volume 2* (Cambridge), pp. 10–38. [Originally 1990]
Skinner, Quentin (2002d). 'Classical Liberty and the Coming of the English Civil War' in Q. Skinner and M. Van Geldren (eds.), *Republicanism: A Shared European Heritage* (Cambridge), pp. 9–28.
Skinner, Quentin (2003). 'States and the Freedom of Citizens' in Q. Skinner and B. Stråth (eds.), *States and Citizens: History, Theory, Prospects* (Cambridge), pp. 11–27.
Skinner, Quentin (2005a). 'The Place of History in Public Life' available at http://www.historyandpolicy.org/papers/policy-paper-35.html . [Accessed 01/10/2009]

Skinner, Quentin (2005b). 'Hobbes on Representation', *European Journal of Philosophy*, 13, pp. 155–184.
Skinner, Quentin (2008a). *Hobbes and Republican Liberty* (Cambridge).
Skinner, Quentin (2008b). 'Freedom as the Absence of Arbitrary Power' in C. Laborde and J. Maynor (eds.), *Republicanism and Political Theory* (Malden), pp. 83–101.
Smith, Adam (1993). *An Enquiry into the Nature and Causes of the Wealth of Nations* (Oxford. Ed. K. Sutherland). [Originally 1776]
Strawson, P.F. (1999). 'Truth' in S. Blackburn and K. Simmons (eds.), *Truth* (Oxford), pp. 162–182. [Originally 1950]
Strawson, P.F. (2004a). 'Intention and Convention in Speech Acts' in Strawson, *Logico-Linguistic Papers* (2nd ed., Aldershot), pp. 115–129. [Originally 1964]
Strawson, P.F. (2004b). 'A Problem About Truth' in Strawson, *Logico-Linguistic Papers* (2nd ed., Aldershot), pp. 165–179. [Originally 1964]
Strawson, P.F. (2004c). 'Meaning and Truth' in Strawson, *Logico-Linguistic Papers* (2nd ed., Aldershot), pp. 131–145. [Originally 1969]
Taylor, Charles (1979). 'What's Wrong with Negative Liberty' in A. Ryan (ed.), *The Idea of Freedom: Essays in Honour of Isaiah Berlin* (Oxford), pp. 175–193.
Thomassen, L. (2007). 'Beyond Representation?' *Parliamentary Affairs*, 60 (1), pp. 111–126.
Tormey, S. (2006). ''Not in My Name': Deleuze, Zapatismo and the Critique of Representation', *Parliamentary Affairs*, 59 (1), pp. 138–154.
Walzer, Michael (1990). 'The Communitarian Critique of Liberalism', *Political Theory*, 18, pp. 6–23.
Williams, Bernard (1972). *Morality: An Introduction to Ethics* (Cambridge).
Williams, Bernard (1981a). 'Moral Luck' in Williams, *Moral Luck: Philosophical Papers 1973–1980* (Cambridge), pp. 20–39. [Originally 1976]
Williams, Bernard (1981b). 'Conflicts of Value' in Williams, *Moral Luck: Philosophical Papers 1973–1980* (Cambridge), pp. 71–82. [Originally 1978]
Williams, Bernard (2005a). 'From Freedom to Liberty: The Construction of a Political Value' in Williams, *In the Beginning Was the Deed* (Princeton. Ed. G. Hawthorne), pp. 75–96. [Originally 2001]
Williams, Bernard (2005b). 'Conflicts of Liberty and Equality' in Williams, *In the Beginning Was the Deed* (Princeton. Ed. G. Hawthorne), pp.115–127.

Williams, Raymond (1965). *The Long Revolution* (London). [Originally 1961]
Williams, Raymond (1983). *Keywords: A Vocabulary of Culture and Society* (New ed., London). [Originally 1976]
Williams, Raymond (1989). 'Democracy and Parliament' in Williams, *Resources of Hope: Culture, Democracy, Socialism* (London), pp. 256–286. [Originally 1982]
Williamson, Timothy (2000). *Knowledge and its Limits* (Oxford).
Wilson, William Julius (1990). *The Truly Disadvantaged: The Inner City, The Underclass and Public Policy* (Chicago).
Wilson, William Julius (1996). *When Work Disappears: The World of the New Urban Poor* (New York).
Wittgenstein, Ludwig (1974). *On Certainty* (New ed. with corr., Oxford. Eds. G.E.M. Anscombe and G.H. Von Wright). [Originally 1949–1951]
Wittgenstein, Ludwig (1980). *Culture and Value* (Chicago. Trans. P. Winch). [Originally 1914–1951]
Wittgenstein, Ludwig (2001). *Philosophical Investigations* (3rd ed., Oxford. Trans. G.E.M. Anscombe). [Originally 1953]
Wolf, Susan (1997). 'Moral Saints' in R. Crisp and M. Slote (eds.), *Virtue Ethics* (Oxford), pp. 79–98. [Originally 1982]
Wolin, Richard (ed.) (1993). *The Heidegger Controversy* (Cambridge, Mass.).
Wiredu, Kwesi. (1996). *Cultural Universals and Particulars: An African Perspective* (Bloomington).
Wiredu, Kwesi. (2001). 'Society and Democracy in Africa' in T. Kiros (ed.), *Explorations in African Political Thought* (London), pp. 171–184.
Žižek, S. (2009). 'How to Begin from the Beginning', *New Left Review*, 57 (May–June).

Index

Akan (Tribe – Ghana), 88
Anarchism, 6, 15, 77, 97
Anarcho-syndicalism, 97
Anscombe, Elizabeth, vii, 105
Apartheid, 116
Aristotle, 70
Asylum seekers, 35, 45
Athens, ix, 41, 49, 80, 91, 101, 102, 112
Austin, J.L., 87 (n.),
Autonomy/autonomous, 35, 84, 85
Ayer, Alfred J., vii, 63–65, 105

Bales, Kevin, 21 (n.)
Barber, Benjamin, 42 (n.)
'Basic Liberties', 17 (n.), 19, 20, 21, 35 (n.), 40, 74, 85, 91–92, 100, 112 (n.), 113, 114
Belief, 8, 30, 31, 39, 51–58, 62, 64, 66, 67, 68, 71–74, 83, 92, 93, 97, 103, 104, 106
Berlin, Isaiah, 8, 17–26, 28, 30, 33–40, 42, 43, 45–50, 52–53, 60, 68, 70–74, 81–82, 84, 89–91, 93, 96, 102, 108–117
Brown, Gordon, 21 (n.), 58 (n.)

Capitalism, 46, 81, 85, 88, 92, 109, 100
Cartledge, Paul, x, 3, 96 (n.), 97 (n.)
Castro, Fidel, 43

Charity, 116
Child-soldiery, 111
Choice, 6–7, 9, 15–21, 23, 24, 26–29, 34, 36, 39, 42, 44, 46–47, 53, 68–70, 72–73, 76–78, 80, 82, 84–85, 88, 94, 97, 101–102, 109–110, 112–116, 118
Cleon, 49,
Coercion, 17, 19–20, 22–23, 28, 35, 37, 40, 59–60, 72–74, 80, 94, 111–116
Cohen, G.A., 79,
Cohen, Leonard, 5,
Co-operation, 1, 3, 5–6, 11, 14, 31, 49, 54, 71, 76–77, 82, 84, 87, 92, 117
'Communalisation of opportunities', 80
Communism, 6, 69, 97
Conceptual scheme, 12, 29, 59, 61, 66, 68, 93, 96
Conflict, 5, 7, 10, 13–15, 36, 58, 61, 67, 84, 92, 111
Conservatism, 6, 15, 35, 36, 45, 77, 91, 99, 117
Constant, Benjamin, 72, 89, 90
Consumerism, 109
Cosmopolitanism, 5, 10, 11, 14, 21, 84

Davidson, Donald, ix, 8–9, 48, 54, 55–56, 58–66, 93, 96, 100, 104–106

Decision Theory, 18 (n.), 101 (n.)
De Gaynesford, Maximilian, 105
Democracy, vii, ix, 8, 10, 12, 15 (n.), 24–25, 40–43, 49, 58–61, 68, 71–72, 75, 76, 80, 84, 97, 101, 108
  Athenian, ix, 40–41, 49,
  Liberal, 24–25, 71–72,
  Participatory, vii, 8, 40–43, 76, 80, 97, 101, 108
  Representative, 40–43, 75–76,
Descartes, Rene, 62 (n.)
Dewey, John, 71 (n.)
'Difference Principle' (Rawls), 31, 86, 110
Disability, 23
  Social model of, 23
Diversity, 13, 41, 81, 109, 114, 117
Dworkin, Ronald, 71, 74–79, 83, 91

Efficiency, 85, 86, 87, 89, 109, 117
'Egalitarian Equal Liberty', 11, 81, 98, 110, 115
Elliot, Jonathan, 42,
Empowerment, 91
Engels, Friedrich, 69
Epistemology, 1, 8–9
Equality, 3, 12, 14, 17, 18, 24, 29, 30, 31, 60, 68, 70, 74–79, 85 (n.), 86, 92, 95, 96, 106, 109–112, 114–116
Evidence, 21, 46, 48, 56, 57, 60, 65, 68, 88, 92, 104, 110
Exploitation, 90, 92

'Fabric of the world' (Mackie), 63, 65, 66
Fairness, 18, 96, 115
  (see also 'Justice as Fairness')
'False consciousness', 59, 61, 68
Fichte, Johann Gottlieb, 34, 43

First-Person Authority, 48–51, 94, 103, 105, 118
Fontana, Biancamaria, 38 (n.), 89 (n.)
Franco, Francisco, 92
Freedom (*See entry for* 'Liberty')
Frege, Gottlob, 69–70

Gandhi, Mahatma, 96
Goody, Jack, 96 (n.)
Green, Thomas Hill, 34

Habermas, Jurgen, 5, 10 (n.)
Hamilton, Alexander, 42 (n.)
Happiness, 6, 13, 19, 28, 29, 38, 39, 47, 76, 77, 81, 86, 92, 107, 113, 115
Harris, Ian, 46
Hart, Herbert L.A., 115–116
Harvey, F.D., 70
Heidegger, Martin, 37 (n.), 38 (n.), 105
Herakleides, 116
Hirschmann, Nancy, 26 (n.)
Hitler, Adolf, 47, 92
Holmes, Stephen, 76 (n.), 81 (n.), 87–88, 109–110
Homelessness, 21, 45, 109
Human flourishing, 117
Human nature, 47, 74, 82, 83, 86, 89, 96, 97 (n.), 109, 110, 117
Human trafficking, 111
Hume, David, 63–64

Intersubjectivity, 12, 55, 61–69

Jay, John, 42 (n.)
Jefferson, Thomas, 6, 13, 43 (n.), 71
Judgement, 7, 11, 31, 46, 47, 50, 51, 53, 55, 61, 63, 64, 65, 69, 92, 93, 94, 101, 103, 104, 106, 119

Index

Justice, 2, 3, 4, 5, 6, 10, 11, 14, 17, 18, 29, 42, 47, 51, 52, 58, 59, 61, 65, 68, 74, 75 (n.), 76, 78, 84, 85, 86, 90, 95, 96, 99, 102, 103, 106, 110, 115, 116
'Justice as fairness' (Rawls), 84, 90
'Political' conception of (Rawls), 2, 11, 84, 86

Kant, Immanuel, 5, 10, 34, 63, 104
Kramer, Matthew, 87,
Kropotkin, Peter, 97 (n.)

Labour, 31, 60, 79, 86, 89, 90, 117
Language, 3, 9, 12, 22 (n.), 29, 38, 43, 46, 50, 51–107, 118
Language-picture, 3 (n.), 51, 52, 53, 61, 67, 68, 88, 90, 92, 93, 96, 103, 106
Political and moral, 51, 65 (n.), 93, 94
Liberalism, 36, 70–78, 81, 83, 87, 117
Liberty, 2, 3, 4 (n.), 6, 7–11, 12 13–32, 33–37, 38, 39, 40, 46, 47, 49, 50, 53, 58, 59, 60, 61, 65, 70, 71, 72, 73, 74, 77, 78, 79, 80, 81, 82, 83, 86, 87, 88, 89, 91, 92, 93, 94, 95, 96, 97, 98, 99, 100, 101, 102, 103, 106, 108, 109, 110, 111, 112, 113, 114, 115, 116, 117, 118, 119
Egalitarian concept of, 11, 98, 108–110, 115
Epistemological, 39, 102–103, 105
Democratic concept of, 40–41, 49, 80, 102, 108–109
Negative, 17 (n.), 33–37, 40, 41, 50, 59 (n.), 71, 78–80, 108–109, 114–115

Neo-classical concept of, 9
Of movement, 35
Positive, 8–9, 15 (n.), 18 (n.), 33–50, 52, 71, 82, 83–92, 102–103, 105, 109, 116, 118
Spectrum of, 95
'Linguistic division of labour' (Putnam), 57, 59
Livingston, Paisley, 105 (n.)

MacCallum, Gerald C., 46 (n.)
Mackie, John L., 63, 66
Madison, James, 41, 42 (n.), 43
Mandela, Nelson, 116, 117
Manin, Bernard, 43 (n.)
Martin, Bill, 63,
Marx, Karl, 39, 69, 87, 115, 116
Mathematics, 65 (n.), 66, 67
Meaning, 3 (n.), 8, 9, 12, 59, 61, 73, 74, 76 (n.), 90, 93, 112 (n.), 118, 119
Messi, Lionel, 26–27
Metz, Thaddeus, 96
Mill, John Stuart, 19 (n.), 35, 50, 71, 72, 101
Miller, David, 109 (n.)
Milton, John, 117
Morality, 34, 69, 72, 78, 88, 94, 105, 111
Objective nature of, 63–69, 104–107
Motivation, 7, 74, 83, 86, 109, 110
Murder, 111
Mussolini, Benito, 43 (n.), 47, 92

'Naturalisation of political philosophy', 47, 50, 51, 93–98, 99, 105
Nazi Germany, 38 (n.), 39
Neurath, Otto, 55
Neutrality, 69–83
Normative concepts, 9, 12, 22, 51, 53, 54, 57, 60, 61, 65, 68, 70, 73, 90, 93, 95, 104, 106

Objectivity, 60–69, 104–107
Oppression, 13, 22, 40, 47, 73, 111, 112, 114
'Original Position' (Rawls), 2–3, 4, 6, 63, 85, 86
Orwell, George, 100
Ostension, 60
Oswald, John, 48 (n.)
'Overlapping Consensus' (Rawls), 11

Paine, Thomas, 118, 119,
Peace, 2, 4, 5, 6, 8, 10–14, 29, 35, 38, 39, 47, 89, 95, 99, 102, 106, 115
  Perpetual, 5, 10–11
Peron, Juan, 43 (n.)
Perikles, 49,
Pettit, Philip, 22 (n.),
Philosophy, 53, 62 (n.), 64, 105
  Central questions of political philosophy, 1, 10, 12, 20 (n.), 28, 78, 83, 94, 118
  Of language, 1, 8
  Political and moral, 1, 7, 8, 9, 10, 12, 20 (n.), 28, 29, 47, 50, 51, 53, 57, 78, 83, 93–98, 99, 105, 106, 118, 119
Pistorius, Oscar, 24
Pitkin, Hanna, 43 (n.)
Plantinga, Carl, 105 (n.)
Plato, 34, 36, 37, 40–41, 49
Plotke, David, 42–44
Plutarch, 116
Pogge, Thomas, 21 (n.), 111 (n.)
Poverty, 20–21, 23, 49, 115–116
Prejudice, 8, 21, 31, 39, 52, 53, 70, 72, 74, 83, 92, 93, 94, 96, 97, 101, 118
Propositions, 55 (n.), 62, 64, 65 (n.)
Psychology, 36, 74, 86, 117
Putnam, Hilary, 55, 57, 59, 66 (n.)

Quine, Willard Van Orman, 9, 47, 55 (n.), 57 (n.), 59 (n.), 60, 61, 66, 67, 92

Railton, Peter, 105,
Ramsey, Frank, 101,
Rape, 111
Rationality, 9, 12, 31, 36, 37, 40, 41, 46, 47, 48, 51–107, 118
Rawls, John, 1–7, 10–12, 13, 14 (n.), 25 (n.), 31, 52, 71, 72, 76 (n.), 77, 78, 82, 84–87, 90–91, 94, 101 (n.), 104, 105, 106, 110, 114 (n.), 115
Refugees, 35 (n.)
Resources, 25 (n.), 31, 60, 75, 77, 79, 117
Rights, 17, 19, 20, 21, 23 (n.), 40, 41, 46, 58, 68, 74, 81, 89, 101, 112, 113, 114
Roberts, Jennifer Tolbert, 40 (n.), 101 (n.)
Rorty, Richard, 62, 71 (n.)
Rousseau, Jean-Jacques, 34, 43, 103

Science, 57, 66, 67
Sen, Amartya, 111 (n.)
Sentences, 55, 60, 61, 65 (n.)
Shah, Idries, 105,
Skinner, Quentin, 3 (n.), 5, 9, 34, 53, 57 (n.), 58, 59 (n.), 66, 67, 68 (n.), 70, 99
Slavery, 21, 116
  'Economic slavery' 19, 20, 74
Socrates, 36
Stalin, Josef, 47, 92
Statements, 46, 55 (n.), 56–57, 65 (n.), 67, 76 (n.), 87–90
Sundarban, 111 (n.)

'Third dogma of empiricism' (Davidson), 59 (n.)
Thomassen, Lasse, 43, 45

Index

Thucydides, 49,
Tormey, Simon, 43
Triangulation (Davidson), 8, 48, 62, 66, 103, 105
Truth, 55–56, 62, 64, 65 (n.), 66–67, 70, 71, 88
'Tyranny of the majority' 101, 102

Values, 2–3, 5, 8–9, 18, 24 (n.), 51–54, 57, 62–68, 72, 76, 81, 83, 84, 87, 104–107
'Veil of Ignorance' (Rawls), 2, 6, 43, 85

Vlassopoulos, Kostas, 31 (n.)
Vocabulary, 61

Walzer, Michael, 71
Well-being, 7, 81, 86, 88
Williams, Bernard, vii, 116–117
Wilson, William Julius, 21 (n.)
Wiredu, Kwasi, 88, 96
Wittgenstein, Ludwig, 48, 51, 53, 57, 60, 87, 119
Words, 8, 21, 55–56, 58–59, 60, 61, 105